Are You Tired of Tenants, Toilets, and Trash?

Jeff Bangerter

The information contained in this book is intended to be educational and not for diagnosis, prescription or treatment of any health disorder whatsoever. This book is sold with the understanding that neither the author nor publisher is engaged in rendering any legal, psychological or accounting advice. The publisher and author disclaim personal liability, directly or indirectly, for advice of information presented within. Although the author and publisher have prepared this manuscript with utmost care and diligence and have made every effort to ensure the accuracy and completeness of the information contained within, we assume no responsibility for errors, inaccuracies, omissions or inconsistencies.

ISBN-13: 978-0-9990232-9-7
Printed in the United States of America

For more information about special discounts for bulk purchases, please contact 3L Publishing at 916.300.8012 or log onto our website at www.3LPublishing.com.

Table of Contents

Introduction

Before taking a deep dive into 1031 exchanges and syndicated real estate investments, I'd like to introduce myself and my background. I started in the financial services industry officially in 1979 and in real estate the year before, in 1978. I cut my teeth working for a title insurance company. In 1979, I started working for Wells Fargo's mortgage company and acquired my real estate license. If you remember 1979, you'll recall that interest rates were high and moving higher every day. I had to come into work and tell people they no longer qualified for their mortgages. In those days, one could have a $50,000 mortgage to buy an $80,000 house, but with 15 to 18% interest rates, it definitely priced people out of the market.

After seeing so many people not able to qualify for a new home and unable to reach their goals, I wanted to engage with clients at a deeper level by helping them plan for their future without being afraid they would be taken advantage of. So, late in 1979 and in early 1980, I decided to get involved in the full financial services industry. I got my insurance license and later my securities license, and I have continued to add licenses along the way. At this point in time, I have a Series 7 registered representative registration, which in lay terms is the stockbroker license; a Series 24 registered principal registration, which means that I can manage other stockbrokers; and a Series 65, which is the license required of an investment adviser representative. I have my insurance license and my real estate license, and I am a licensed mortgage loan originator. I also have my own firm, which is a California-registered investment advisory firm. Additionally, a few years ago, I decided to get my enrolled agent tax professional license to make sure that I understood the tax consequences of the various investment strategies we use, though I do not do individual taxes.

Early in my career, I was taught to take care of my own clients and recruit other financial professionals to the various companies I represented, training them in these unique products and their uses. In the late 1980s, a partner and I had the largest life insurance marketing company with Hartford Life. We transitioned into recruiting advisers to market fixed-indexed annuities with a variety of companies.

In 2002, I heard about a new securitized real estate program that would allow real estate investors to do a 1031 exchange into a tenant-in-common real estate portfolio. With my long history and connection to the real estate industry along with my securities registration, this was a niche that had great appeal to me.

I started working with my own clients who had investment real estate that they wanted to sell, and we were able to provide replacement property for 1031 exchanges through the tenant-in-common program. However, there were some issues with this strategy. One weakness that the tenant-in-common program had was that you could only have up to 35 investors in one property, and everyone had to agree to any changes or when or if the property were to be sold. So even if you had a great offer and everyone was going to make substantial capital gains, one owner could prevent the sale of the property. This weakness has been remedied with the new Delaware statutory trust (DST).

My goal in writing this book is to give you a simplified version of how the 1031 to DST tax-deferred exchange works, while providing enough detail to allow you to move forward to make this type of investment if it makes sense for your personal financial situation.

A Quick Overview

Among the things that successful real estate investors need to know are how to pick the right property and how to negotiate a favorable sale price. Add another item to the list: the 1031 exchange. This tax rule is an extremely powerful tool for real estate investors. The complexities of a 1031 exchange, however, mean that many investors don't have a full understanding of how this tool works or how best to take advantage of its important tax benefits.

To make the most of a 1031 exchange, it's important to get up to speed on how it works. Let's start at the beginning: Since 1921, the Internal Revenue Service has allowed 100% of realized gains from property sales to be deferred in a code section 1031 exchange. Here's how the IRS describes a 1031 exchange:

> No gain or loss shall be recognized on the exchange of property held for productive use in a trade or business or for investment purposes if such property is exchanged solely for property of like-kind, which is to be held for the productive use in trade or business or for investment purposes.

In short, if an investor sells a property and uses the proceeds to buy another similar property, they can defer capital gains and losses indefinitely, or at least until they make a final sale of a property.

The ability to defer taxes is the key benefit of a 1031 exchange. All taxpaying entities are entitled to the benefits of section 1031, including individuals, corporations, partnerships, limited liability companies, trusts and even non-U.S. citizens who own property in the United States. The 1031 exchange allows investors to buy new property without losing purchasing power to capital gains tax. And the exchange provides flexibility in the types of properties that investors can buy, as long as the property is held as an investment or to produce income.

In addition, an investor can exchange one property for another single property or multiple properties and vice versa. They may also invest in securitized real estate (discussed below), which provides investors with additional options and benefits that are unavailable through traditional real estate. Investors may exchange the full equity from a sale for a 100% tax deferral on the exchange. Or if they decide to exchange only a portion of the equity from a sale, investors may pay taxes on the portion that is not exchanged.

To make an exchange, investors must acquire a like-kind property of equal or greater value and equal or greater debt. The investor must identify and purchase a replacement property within a strict time frame and use an intermediary to make the exchange.

Here's what investors need to know to gain a foundational understanding of how this powerful tool works.

What is a like-kind property? Any real property located in the United States or its territories that is held for productive use in a trade or business or for investment is considered like-kind property. Examples of like-kind property include securitized real estate, condominiums, raw land, apartments, single-family homes, industrial property, retail properties, duplexes, office space, storage facilities, medical buildings, or student housing. Property that is not like-kind property includes shares of stock, a personal residence, real estate investment trusts (REITs), property outside the United States, land held for inventory, interests in a partnership, or a mortgage carry-back structure.

Pursuant to The Tax Cuts and Jobs Act of 2017 signed into law by President Donald Trump on December 22, 2017 (most of the changes introduced by the bill went into effect on January 1, 2018, and do not affect 2017 taxes), the ability to enter into a 1031 Exchange for any asset other than real estate was eliminated. Consequently, a 1031 Exchange will not apply to the extent an investor is disposing of property that does not qualify as real estate or to the extent that a portion of the property consists of property other than real estate. We note that some have taken the position that the aforementioned change in the 1031 Exchange law is applicable to only direct exchanges of personal property and not to nominal personal property tied to a real estate exchange; however, we note that there is no written authority that allows nominal personal property tied to real estate to be exchanged under the current 1031 Exchange law.

Therefore, it is possible that personal property tied to an otherwise real estate 1031 Exchange (for example, refrigerators, ranges, washers, and dryers found within the units of an apartment property), may not be exchanged under the current 1031 Exchange law and therefore, may be subject to taxation.

What is the time frame? After selling a property, investors must identify a specific potential replacement property or properties within 45 days of closing. They must then acquire the replacement property or properties within 180 days of closing the relinquished property or by the due date of their tax return for the year of transfer of the relinquished property, whichever occurs first. There are no extensions for any reason, except if offered by the government following a natural disaster.

Within the initial 45-day period, investors must follow certain guidelines for identifying properties. They may choose to follow one of three rules:

The three-property rule allows investors to identify a maximum of three replacement properties without regard to fair market value. Investors typically purchase only one of the properties, and the other two exist as backup in case the first property cannot be acquired.

The 200% rule lets investors identify any number of properties as long as their total fair market value does not exceed 200% of the total fair market value of the relinquished property.

The 95% rule allows investors to identify any number of replacement properties, but they must purchase 95% of all identified properties. When investors make an identification, it must be in writing and signed by the investor before midnight of the 45th day. The identification must be unambiguous, having a specific property address. An identification may be revoked within the 45-day period, but investors are still required to have a replacement property within the original 45 days.

What is the role of an intermediary? The IRS requires that 1031 exchanges use an independent, unrelated qualified intermediary (QI) to act as the middleman for the purpose of acquiring and transferring relinquished and replacement properties. The QI may also be called an accommodator or facilitator.

Investors should choose an experienced, insured or bonded, and financially stable company to act as QI, as the QI will hold money from the sale of the relinquished property before the purchase of a new property. The QI additionally performs these duties:

- provides the required exchange agreement and the exchange addendum for the relinquished and replacement properties

- accepts the assignment of relinquished and replacement property contracts

- provides notification of the assignments to all parties

- furnishes instructions to settlement agents

- establishes qualified escrow accounts to hold the proceeds from the relinquished property

- delivers escrow funds for the replacement property settlement

- provides the final accounting

A QI typically charges around $1,000 regardless of the value of the property.

How much tax is deferred? A 1031 exchange helps defer a number of taxes that the sale of a property would otherwise incur. First and foremost, investors defer federal and state capital gains tax. In 2018, the federal capital gains rate was 15 or 20%, depending on an investor's tax bracket. State capital gains tax varies by state but can also be high. In California, a high-tax state, the capital gains tax rate was between 9 and 13% in 2018. The seller may be liable for depreciation recapture as well. For most investors who have used depreciation on a property they own to offset income tax, the IRS requires that they repay the depreciation after selling the property at a rate of 25%. As of 2018, investors must pay a net investment income tax of 3.8% if an investor's adjusted gross income is over $200,000 for a single person or $250,000 for a couple.

The bottom line: Without a 1031 exchange, a property could be subject to a blended tax rate near 45% if the seller lives in a higher-taxed state.

The role of securitized real estate. In some cases, investors may be ready to sell an investment property but may not be prepared to buy another property or properties on their own. Securitized real estate provided through a sponsor company gives investors the opportunity to own shares of real estate while still qualifying for a 1031 exchange. There are two common forms of securitized real estate that investors may encounter: tenant-in-common (TIC) ownership and Delaware statutory trusts (DSTs).

Tenant-in-common ownership. TIC ownership is a form of acquiring and owning real estate with multiple owners through undivided fractional interests. The IRS acknowledged TICs in 2002 through revenue procedure 2002–22. Each owner receives his or her own deed and the full benefits of ownership, and generally qualifies for a 1031 exchange. TIC property offers individual investors access to commercial properties otherwise typically acquired by institutional investors, such as REITs, pension funds and insurance companies.

TIC ownership offers a number of potential advantages. First, TICs are flexible. They offer pre-packaged replacement property alternatives and an easy solution to help investors meet the 45-day property identification period. In addition to helping investors meet exchange deadlines, TICs are easy to match to investors' equity and debt. TICs offer investors the ability to exchange property for institutional quality properties and a way for investors to transition from actively managed properties, like rentals, to passive management.

Investors are entitled to a pro rata portion of potential appreciation of the property held through the TIC structure. They are also able to be active in certain major decision-making opportunities surrounding TIC leasing, financing, management and the sale of the property. TICs can be used in estate-planning strategies and sold to do future 1031 exchanges.

TIC ownership does have some potential disadvantages, however, such as a lack of liquidity and a potentially high required investment amount due to a TIC ownership cap of 35 investors.

Decision-making among 35 owners can be difficult if the owners do not share the same opinions. For example, if a majority of investors want to exit the TIC but one owner chooses not to, everyone must hold the asset until all owners are ready to sell. Investors who hold TICs may risk overconcentration on a single asset, and there may be additional fees and expenses associated with holding shares.

Delaware statutory trusts. A second form of securitized real estate that can be useful in 1031 exchanges is the Delaware statutory trust. IRS ruling 2004–86 distinguished the DST from limited partnership interests and created it as a 1031 exchange option. The DST is a limited purpose entity, which can hold title to real property. Property can be co-owned through beneficial interests, and active management of real assets is delegated by DST lease contracts. Debt is allocated pro rata for exchange purposes, and the active management must be conducted outside of the trust.

The DST ownership structure offers the following advantages. First, there are no explicit limits on the number of co-owners, so investment amounts can be lower than with a TIC. If borrowing money to acquire a property, the DST acts as one entity. Lenders deal directly with the DST and don't require a credit review of any co-owners. DSTs may make it easier to sell investment interests to third-party investors, since lenders don't have to approve the sale. Additionally, there are lower investor and sponsor transaction costs due to less investor paperwork.

The potential disadvantages of DST ownership include the fact that DST powers limit the trustee's ability to add capital or take on additional debt for a property. The trustee, or master lessee, must take responsibility for fixing unforeseen problems, and beneficial interests don't convey voting rights in management decisions.

There are other DST limitations—commonly known as "the seven deadly sins"—that investors should take into consideration. According to IRS ruling 2004–86, for beneficial interest to qualify as direct interest in real estate for section 1031 purposes, the DST may not engage in these actions:

- exchange DST property for other property

- invest cash between distribution dates in anything other than short-term securities

- accept additional capital to the DST

- renegotiate terms of debt or enter into new financing

- renegotiate existing leases

- enter into new leases

- make repairs or improvements other than minor, non-structural repairs

If case one of these prohibitions must be performed, DSTs do contain provisions that allow conversion into a limited liability company taxed as a partnership. Such a change is normally not taxable, but it may limit future 1031 exchange options. Some of these restrictions actually provide advantages as well. For example, since the DST cannot borrow additional capital, it provides a natural endpoint for the project. If the DST has provisions for 10-year financing, the sponsor company will be motivated to sell the project in that time frame.

How and why are TICs and DSTs generally offered as securities? When entering into a TIC or DST, investors are purchasing a complete financial package or arrangement. Investors rely on the expertise of the sponsor company to provide a good investment. For this reason, and because investors are investing money in common enterprises with the expectation of a profit,

TICs and DSTs meet the definition of an investment contract or securities.

Securities are sold through broker-dealers who are registered and governed by the Financial Industry Regulatory Authority, the Securities and Exchange Commission, and state securities commissions. Securities have disclosure requirements and a private placement memorandum, and the sponsor or seller is subject to the antifraud regulations of the Securities Act of 1933.

The role of a securities broker is to advise and represent the investor regarding suitable investment alternatives and to perform due diligence on private real estate investment offerings through a team of licensed professionals. The securities representative works for the investors, consulting with them to determine suitable properties to meet their particular risk tolerance and investment, and tax and estate-planning needs. They have access to a variety of institutional-grade, triple-net master leases or long-term investment properties.

In contrast, real estate is sold through real estate brokers who are governed by state and local departments of real estate and are not required to provide full disclosure, except on known property conditions.

- Who qualifies for securitized real estate ownership? Securitized real estate programs are not available to everyone—there are limitations in place to protect investors. TICs and DSTs can typically only be offered to accredited investors, which means investors must have either a net worth of $1 million (excluding the worth of their home and personal items) or an annual income in excess of $200,000 or $300,000 for joint investors. The property must be suitable for each investor's individual situation. And investors and their advisers must understand what the investor's tax obligation will be before they are allowed to purchase securitized real estate. Note Rule 506 States: "The company may sell its securities to an unlimited number of "accredited investors" and up to 35 other purchasers. All non-accredited investors, either alone or with a purchaser representative, must be sophisticated—that is, they must have sufficient knowledge and experience in financial and business matters to make them capable of evaluating the merits and risks of the prospective investment." I have not seen a broker-dealer firm allow a non-accredited investor into one of these investments, but the law does have some provisions for it.

The role of the real estate sponsor. Both DSTs and TICs are offered through real estate sponsors. Sponsors are typically an experienced real estate company that researches the market; locates investment properties; arranges for the property's purchase, financing and management; and then offers shares to multiple 1031 exchange co-owners. Sponsors process cash-flow disbursements to investors and provide regular investor reports. Ultimately, the sponsor coordinates the property sale and provides investors with their portions of the proceeds.

Though sponsors make DST and TIC opportunities possible, there are a few drawbacks. They are the decision-makers, so investors may have limited decision-making abilities. Sponsors may have conflicts of interest, and their choices may have negative impacts on the investment. There may be additional fees associated with using a sponsor.

However, it is this sponsorship structure that provides 1031 exchange investors an opportunity to own a portion of a large property that would otherwise be out of reach for many of them. Sponsors also provide an avenue for active real estate investors to transition into passive ownership and provide real estate expertise typically afforded to institutional investors only.

Considering the due diligence and reviews that are done to facilitate DST and TIC arrangements, these investment structures can, in many ways, be a better way to own real estate than if investors were to shop for and manage a rental property on their own.

With this basic understanding of how 1031 exchanges work and the investment options available through them, let's take a deeper look at DSTs specifically, the players involved and the specific potential benefits of investing in securitized real estate.

Securitized Real Estate Basics: Delaware Statutory Trusts

Every day, I help people make decisions about their futures and retirements, and as part of that process, when suitable, I often help place major portions of clients' net worth in real estate. While many clients already understand direct investment in real estate, I spend a lot of time educating new clients about the obscure world of syndicated real estate, with a focus on (DSTs). These programs allow a group of investors to pool their money and access large properties that might otherwise be available to institutional investors only. These investments can be extremely useful when coupled with a 1031 exchange strategy. Before having clients invest in a DST, however, I take a very slow, methodical approach to educating them so they know exactly what they're getting into and feel a sense of confidence in any decision they may make.

The goal in making syndicated real estate investments like DSTs is to build a diversified real estate portfolio, one that at the least, defers capital gains taxes and is managed by experts who take the onus of real estate management off the investor. A syndicated real estate portfolio should spin off a healthy and predictable cash flow that is largely sheltered from taxes. Properties should appreciate over time, and when they are sold, investors can choose new properties to purchase through a 1031 exchange. Investors can do this indefinitely even up until their deaths. At that point, it's possible that their heirs won't have to pay all of the capital gains tax accumulated over the years of ownership. Under current tax law, they'll get a step up in the cost basis upon the investor's death and no one will be responsible for the capital gains tax.

The securitized real estate industry is very heavily regulated for the good reason that regulation protects investors. The Securities and Exchange Commission and the Financial Industry Regulatory Authority regulate every investment that I recommend to my clients. When I meet with investors to discuss investment options, I must use fair and balanced language—for every positive, I must present a negative. See Appendix IV for a list of many of the risks that owning securitized real estate presents.

Before getting deeper into DSTs, here's a look at a common direct real estate investment that investors may already hold—rental property.

Rental Property
For the most part, investors are probably already familiar with the concept of rental property. They can purchase a house or apartment building, manage it, and collect rent from tenants. Rental properties produce a steady stream of income, and the property may also appreciate, giving the owner a gain when they eventually sell it. There are some important things to keep in mind when making this type of direct investment.

Diversification and property selection. It behooves investors to own properties diversified beyond one town or county, as non-diversified real estate puts investors at risk. For example, consider properties that are all in one geographical area that is supported largely by one local industry, like technology or the military. If the bottom falls out of the industry, investors may find themselves with severely depreciated property values as people leave the area. It's much safer to spread real estate investments over multiple, carefully selected geographical locations and varied types of real estate than to keep one high-value property. Diversify among towns with multiple industries, above-average population growth and above-average income growth. These factors alone lower the risk, and combining all three is a winning strategy for lowering risk.

Secondary income streams. In addition to rent, secondary income streams—such as rental washer and dryers, pet fees and storage-room fees—can provide steady cash flow. Yet, without the requisite knowledge to set up secondary income streams, most people don't consider it.

Property management. Some people love managing investment properties—they enjoy fixing toilets, installing smoke detectors, and mowing lawns. For others, managing property is a necessary evil. A tenant leaves after 10 years, and it's time to break out the checkbook and put $20,000 into the property, hire contractors, and go through the process of finding a new tenant, hoping the next tenant pays the rent on time and doesn't trash the place.

In many cases, institutional property investment can address these considerations more easily than investors can on their own through direct investments. Investing in shares of properties allows investors to diversify across geographical areas and markets. And professional managers oversee the properties, including secondary income streams and the day-to-day management of buildings and tenants.

Syndicated real estate as an alternative to direct investment
Investors can use 1031 exchanges to move capital from direct investments to beneficial interests in a DST. The 1031 exchange allows investors to defer taxes when they sell one property and buy other investment properties. This tax advantage means that investors defer carving out a chunk of the sale to give to Uncle Sam and can invest the entire amount made on the sale

into new property.

The tax implications of selling an investment property can be devastating, and the fear of it often keeps people from selling at all. Capital gains tax will take 15 to 40% of the gain when a property is sold, making it very difficult to continue to build estate investments. By using a 1031 exchange, investors no longer have to be afraid that when selling an asset, a large portion of the profits will go to the government.

Why Syndicated Real Estate is Important

DSTs are legal structures that allow smaller real estate investors to access large institutional-grade properties by contributing to their equity along with a group of other investors. DSTs are offered and managed by firms called sponsor companies, which perform many functions on behalf of the investors. The benefit to the investor is a hands-off management, prepackaged real estate investment that provides the potential for annual net cash flows, which have historically ranged from 5 to 7%, with potential appreciation and use of depreciation to shelter current income. DST investors can close a purchase within a matter of days with no closing costs.

The other advantage of purchasing a DST is that investors gain access to a class A property, whether in the form of a student housing project at a prestigious college, a beautiful apartment complex, medical facilities leased out to large corporate medical companies, or retail space guaranteed by some of the largest corporations in the world. That investor would have the advantage of continuing to own real estate, which generally experiences less volatility than investments in the stock market.

Investors may worry that they'll be missing out on capital appreciation if they invest in a DST, but this is not the case. Every five to 10 years, on average, the properties in a DST are sold. At that point, investors can either cash out or do another 1031 exchange with the new increased amount of cash. If the investor chooses to make a 1031 exchange, all of this money will go to work for them.

Focusing on Rate of Return

In my experience, rental property owners often think they're getting pretty good cash flow or rate of return from their investments in real estate, but most are not. They often have a large portion of their net worth in one or two pieces of real estate in the same area, which is risky. In Sacramento, where I live, the average home price in 2018 is around $500,000, and an average rent is around $2,000 a month, which would generate a 4.8% rate of return before taxes, repairs and other costs. The real rate of return after costs is significantly less. Investors must factor in the cost of the time it takes to manage the property, repair the property, and lease out the property. If using a professional management company, investors also need to reduce the rate of return by the amount they're paying the management company. The sponsors of DSTs take care of these issues, and the net rate of return has historically ranged between 5 and 7% in today's market. Let's look at a hypothetical example:

Imagine an investor had a rental house worth $1 million with no debt in the Sacramento market. Subtracting roughly $70,000 for closing costs on a potential sale, there would be $930,000 of equity tied up in the property. Now, let's say the investor bought that house 30 years ago for $80,000 and is now charging $2,500 a month for rent. That would provide a 3% rate of return on the $1 million, which may only cover taxes and repairs. Now, if the investors decided to be done being landlords and carried out a 1031 exchange into a DST that was generating a mere 5% cash-on-cash return, they would increase their cash flow potential to $3,875 a month and would have no upkeep, no taxes and no tenants to deal with.

Let's say the same investors decided to sell the property and invest the after-tax money in a mutual fund or some other investment that generated a 5% rate of return. The property sale would generate a number of taxes. First, let's imagine the house had depreciation recapture of $70,000. The investor would owe a tax of 25%, or $17,500, on the recapture. Next, the investor would have to pay federal capital gains tax. If we assume the lowest bracket of 15%, the investor would pay an additional $127,500. There may also be state taxes. In California, capital gains tax is between 9 and 13%. At the 9% rate, the investors would owe an additional $76,500 in taxes for a total tax bill of $221,500. So the net after taxes from the sale of the property would be $708,500. Assuming a 5% return, the investors would receive a monthly income of $2,952 a month, or $923 per month less after taxes than they would make with the 1031 exchange into a DST.

It's important to evaluate the true rate of return on investments and structure retirement investments to meet the desired lifestyle. Does a 75- or 80-year-old rental property owner really want to be going out and fixing leaky faucets or broken air conditioner units? What does it cost in time and money to maintain a property? A DST may have the potential to help provide more money to help investors meet their retirement goals while freeing up time so they can enjoy their goals.

The Tax Advantages of a 1031 Exchange

One of the greatest challenges facing active real estate investors who are interested in selling their properties and moving into a passive ownership role is the tax implication of that sale.

There are a host of liabilities that amount to, what can be, a very substantial final tax bill:

- Federal and state taxes. In most states, real estate sales are taxed at both the state and federal level. Depending upon your income, federal rates range between 15% and 20%, while state taxes range between 9% and 13%. In California, which has one of the highest state tax rates, that blended tax rate on the sale of a property could average between 33% and 35%.

- Medicare surtax. If you have an adjusted gross income of $250,000 or more, you're obligated to pay a 3.8% net investment tax—the so-called Medicare tax—on your property sale.

- Depreciation recapture. Though it's often overlooked, depreciation recapture—levied at a rate of 25%—is the highest individual tax an investor will pay on the sale of a property. The tax is based on the total amount of depreciation that you've taken on your rental real estate over the life of the investment. When you own an income property, the tax code allows you to deduct the annual depreciation on your building to help offset the taxes due on rental income. But when you sell the property, the portion of the gain that is equal to the deductions you've claimed is subject to recapture. Say you've owned a rental property for 10 years, and in that time, you've claimed a total of $25,000 in deductions for depreciation. If you sell the property for a gain of $100,000, $25,000 is taxed at the recapture rate of 25% and the remaining $75,000 is taxed at the capital gains rate of 20%.

In all, a real estate owner can safely assume that upward of a third of what they make on the sale of an investment property will go to paying taxes. Given that the liability can cost investors tens or hundreds of thousands of dollars, the value of a 1031 exchange is clear. By swapping like-assets rather than liquidating them, investors can defer taxes, retain their equity, and roll it into other more valuable real estate investments.

A Tool for Building—and Preserving—Wealth
Using a 1031 exchange to defer tax liability on the sale of property allows you to leverage the returns you've generated through real estate into investments with even better return potential. (See hypothetical examples on pages 48 and 49.) This is especially true of DSTs, which allow investors to roll proceeds from the sale of smaller individually managed properties into shares of larger higher-quality—and potentially higher-yielding—institutional projects. This tax strategy has the potential to help investors quickly and efficiently build wealth, allowing them to compound returns rather than pass a substantial percentage of them along to the government. Reinvesting proceeds through a 1031 exchange not only provides owners with the potential for greater monthly income but greater gains when those properties are eventually resold.

In addition to helping investors grow their estates, the mechanics of a 1031 exchange can also help investors facilitate an advantageous transfer of those assets to their heirs.

What's important to remember is that 1031 exchanges allow investors to defer—not eliminate—their tax liabilities. Say you perform a series of 1031 exchanges over 30 years and ultimately liquidate the property (or your shares of the property) in question. At the time of that final sale, you must pay taxes on both the accumulated deferred investment gains generated over those three decades as well as the taxes owed on any depreciation recapture benefits you've enjoyed.

Alternatively, the IRS allows you to exchange like-kind properties—and defer taxes on those sales—indefinitely throughout your lifetime. Financial professionals sometimes refer to the strategy as "swap 'til you drop." And there's a substantial benefit in doing so: When an investor passes away without liquidating 1031 exchange assets, the underlying appreciated real estate passes to their heirs tax-free. It's an incredibly powerful estate-planning tool and makes "swap 'til you drop" as much a suggestion to investors as it is a description of the approach.

The inheritor of those appreciated real estate assets has a number of options. If they wish, they can liquidate their DST interest when the DST is sold, incurring zero tax liability on the sale. If they choose to hold onto the assets, their tax basis is reset to the fair market value of the property on the day that it was inherited. Thanks to that step-up in basis, the inheritor is liable only for the taxable gains generated by the asset from that day forward.

Securing a step-up in basis for your heirs is a fantastic way to eliminate the tax liability that you've been deferring through swaps over the course of your lifetime, including any depreciation recapture benefits that you may have used to shield your past income from taxes. Sidestepping capital gains tax completely can increase the size of an inheritance by potentially millions of dollars.

Often, when an heir receives a DST as part of their inheritance, they will leave the investment in place until the property is sold by the sponsor. They can then cash out of the investment or continue using sequential 1031 exchanges to defer their own capital gains taxes.

The "swap-'til-you-drop" provision included in 1031 exchanges provides an exception to the adage that nothing is certain in life but death and taxes. Using this strategy effectively helps investors avoid at least one of those certainties.

To illustrate the compounding power of sequential 1031 exchanges, let's look at a hypothetical client situation.

Richard bought a duplex in 2005 for $1 million, with $500,000 cash and a $500,000 loan. Today, the duplex is worth $1,950,000, and Richard—now on the cusp of retirement and ready to hang up his spurs as a landlord—decides he wants to sell.

He sells the duplex for $1,967,150 and has a total of $1,420,678 in proceeds after the cost of the sale. By rolling that money into a 1031 exchange, Richard avoids roughly $147,000 in capital gains tax (assuming a capital gains rate of 35%). He invests the proceeds from the sale into a DST with a 50% loan-to-value ratio, allowing him to purchase $2,841,356 in property value.

After seven and a half years, Richard's DST investment sells for $3,296,301. His investment of $1,420,678 nets him $1,958,043 after the sale. To calculate his gain, we add his original basis in the duplex he owned ($1 million) to the amount of additional property he bought when he invested in the DST ($1,011,095). That gives him a new basis of $2,011,095. His total capital gain now is $1,284,396.

If Richard decides to take the proceeds from the sale and cash out, his capital gains tax will be approximately $450,000

($1,284,396 x 35%). Instead, Richard reinvests the proceeds into another DST. The new DST also has a 50% loan-to-value ratio, so he now owns $3,916,086 worth of property in the investment.

Sadly, before Richard's second DST sells, he passes away at the age of 75 and leaves the investment property to his son. When the DST does sell months later for a little more than $4,500,000, Richard's original duplex investment of $500,000 has more than quadrupled.

His son inherits the $2,686,240 proceeds from the sale at a stepped-up basis and owes no capital gains tax. Over his 25 years of real estate ownership, Richard accumulated a gain of $1,900,000. Had he lived and cashed out on his investment after the sale, he would have paid $668,998 in capital gains tax.

Using sequential 1031 exchanges, Richard not only generated more annual income from his investment than he would have with the duplex but provided his son with a sizable inheritance as well. A stunning $668,998, which would have otherwise gone to paying taxes, remained in his estate.

Like Richard, many investors can use 1031 exchanges (and the tax benefits they provide) to live progressively better lifestyles as they age and avoid the compromises and discomforts faced by those who find themselves in jeopardy of outliving their retirement funds.

Institutional Investing and the Role of Sponsors

Big institutions like pension funds, real estate investment trusts, banks, hedge funds, insurance companies, university endowments, and foundations invest in real estate very differently than average investors. Institutions can invest in large-scale projects that the average investor—who might otherwise own single-family homes, two- to four-unit buildings, condos or very small apartment buildings—doesn't have access to. Yet, when individual investors pool their resources in a process called real estate syndication, they can invest in attractive real estate properties with the potential for high returns that are usually only available to big institutions.

In the syndicated real estate arena, institutional investments are made accessible to individual investors through firms called sponsors, which offer institutional real estate through DSTs. The size of investments available through DSTs varies. A smaller DST program might offer a $5 million property, while larger programs could offer properties worth in excess of $100 million. Sponsors offer large-scale properties ranging from storage facilities to apartment complexes to big-box retailers to class A office complexes. Investors may have access to projects that don't have a mortgage or projects that use leverage to generate a higher monthly cash flow and provide greater depreciation to offset investors' taxable income.

Here's a look at how sponsors acquire institutional-style properties, and how they offer these properties to investors.

Who Acquires DST Property?

Sponsors typically have decades of highly specialized experience and employ specific strategies to acquire, manage, improve and sell properties for maximum cash flow and profit. A sponsor usually acquires one or more institutional-grade properties of similar type, packages them into a DST structure, and offers them to accredited investors through securities professionals called registered representatives or investment advisers. Sponsors are responsible for getting financing for the property if appropriate.

Once a property is acquired and packaged in a DST, the sponsor then offers a percentage of the ownership to accredited investors. The sponsor manages the property on behalf of the investors until its ultimate sale. When the sponsor sells the property, the investors gain whatever cash flow, appreciation and pay down of loan principal the sponsor was able to achieve over the course of the DST. During that time, depreciation helps shelter annual income from taxes.

How do sponsors choose properties?

Sponsors typically have specific criteria on which they base their selection of properties to purchase. Different sponsors specialize in specific types of real estate. One might focus on retail, another on multifamily apartments or student housing, and another on commercial offices, hotels or senior housing. Specialization in one segment of real estate helps sponsors focus and seek solid and consistent returns from an area they know well. Sponsors apply their expertise to the properties in their sector and work to increase the net operating income of their selected properties.

Sponsors often source the properties they buy off market, meaning they rely on private relationships to seek and acquire property below appraised value.

Most sponsors in the multifamily apartment market buy class A property, which includes high-quality, newer buildings with top amenities and low vacancy rates. The properties are typically in secondary markets. For example, sponsors might look to submarkets outside of major metropolitan areas (such as Phoenix; Austin, Texas; or Nashville, Tennessee) instead of sourcing real estate in a primary market, like San Francisco or Los Angeles. Key criteria for investing in these submarkets includes looking for submarkets that are growing faster than the larger metro market in regard to income and population growth.

How is the property structured?
Recently, sponsors have changed how they typically structure their real estate offerings. Prior to 2008, most syndicated real estate investments were TIC structures with up to 35 individual owners who were also the investors. Each of the owners had decision-making authority on major decisions, which required a majority vote or a unanimous vote. Achieving consensus among many owners proved difficult at times. Additionally, any loan on the property required all the owners to qualify. This system worked, but it was unwieldy during the Great Recession, when property values plummeted. Individual investors in TIC structures did not have the commercial real estate expertise required to manage critical decisions when dealing with failing properties or properties that required loans.

In the syndicated real estate market today, sponsors nearly exclusively use DSTs as their legal structure. Individual investors each own beneficial shares in the trust, but they have no decision-making authority or personal responsibility for the loan on the property. DSTs create a streamlined process in which the sponsors are tasked with managing a property's performance.

Within the structure of DSTs, there are two teams of managers: property managers and asset managers. Property managers may be part of the DST firm or hired from a large, national or regional property management firm. Asset managers are always employees of the sponsor. They design the overall business plan, manage its implementation, and watch the local market for opportunities and threats.

How do investors gain a return?

The foundation of a consistent return is for sponsors to increase net operating income over the life of ownership. Net operating income is total income minus total expenses, and it does not include loan payments. Actions that either increase income or reduce expenses change the net operating income and provide more return for the investors. Some additional benefit to the investors may be achieved via appreciation in the value of the property and pay down of any loan principal.

Increasing income. Sponsors look to increase income in a number of ways. For example, in multifamily apartments, sponsors typically survey market rents daily or weekly and adjust the rental rate for new tenants and lease renewals accordingly. They may use computer modeling to fine-tune rents relative to competitors. Additional sources of income (pet fees, garage and storage rental, and such enhancements as valet trash pickup or utility charge-backs) may add to net income.

Sponsors also institute programs and provide amenities—such as gyms, pools or concierge services—to maximize the attractiveness of their properties to prospective tenants and to retain existing tenants. Today, sponsors pay close attention to the online reputation of the properties they manage. Social-media-savvy sponsors maximize their online presence and employ tactics to get more likes, friends or followers.

Factors like these can add $20 to $200 a month or more to the income derived from each apartment in a building. That increase multiplied by the number of apartments in a complex over the course of a year can dramatically increase net operating income.

Managing expenses. Sponsors scrutinize all expenses carefully and ensure the property is properly maintained. Sponsors minimize expenses largely through economics of scale. They often use the same vendors for all the properties they manage, which gives them access to discounts on such things as insurance, maintenance, suppliers and contractors. Sponsors normally take bids for service contracts every year to secure the best prices. Sponsors closely review property taxes each year to determine whether they need to be appealed.

While this is by no means an exhaustive list of the ways sponsors create value by increasing net operating income; however, these are among the most effective. These cost-management tactics allow sponsors to operate on a more efficient level and on a larger scale than individual investors.

The Role of Realtors and Registered Securities Representatives

Some people may wonder why their real estate professional hasn't presented them with the option of investing through a DST. After all, DSTs are real estate investments, so why wouldn't you hear about it first from your trusted real estate agent? The answer: Realtors and real estate brokers are in the business of buying and selling property, and syndicated real estate investing through DSTs falls outside of their expertise and licensing. So while DSTs are related, they aren't the same as the real estate your realtor might offer. Here's a look at the role that realtors play and how they differ from registered securities representatives who can sell beneficial interests of DSTs.

The Role of Realtors

Realtors assist their clients in buying and selling residential properties, and commercial real estate brokers help investors find apartments and other commercial properties to buy. In a regular 1031 exchange, both kinds of realtors can help investors find replacement properties. However, realtors cannot help investors exchange real estate they own for interests in properties offered through DSTs.

Syndicated real estate is offered as a security, which can only be offered by a properly licensed and registered securities representative or investment adviser. Real estate brokers typically do not hold these licenses and do not have access to the DST market. As a result, few real estate professionals are aware of syndicated real estate as an investment option, and even fewer know the nuances and subtleties of the industry.

You can work with a real estate agent who can help you sell existing property for the highest possible price. And if they are aware of the DST as an investment option, they might be able to refer you to a registered representative or investment adviser who specializes in them.

The Role of Registered Securities Representatives and Investment Advisers

Due to limited control by investors and the fact that a third-party sponsor manages DSTs, federal rules mandate that securities laws must govern the sale of DSTs. Several important consequences result from this requirement. First, DSTs can only be purchased through registered and properly licensed securities dealers. Second, real estate agents and brokers are not able to sell DSTs or receive any compensation that is based on the amount of funds raised. Third, securities dealers are forbidden from sharing any fees with individuals who are not also licensed as securities brokers. This includes prohibitions on providing finders fees to unlicensed individuals.

The SEC has certain standards that must be met by representatives who want to sell securities. Registered representatives must successfully obtain certain securities licenses, such as the Series 7 and Series 63, that allow them to offer DST property. To protect consumers, the SEC further requires that specific, exhaustive disclosures are provided to clients regarding each individual DST offering through the PPM (Private Placement Memorandum).

Often, a group of registered securities representatives will hold their licenses through an entity called a broker-dealer, who is involved in the marketing and sales of DST offerings. The broker-dealer supervises the registered representatives and provides back-end support on securities-related matters. They analyze and provide due diligence on DST sponsor companies and their DSTs before their registered representatives offer them to investors.

When a broker-dealer determines that a particular DST property is appropriate to offer to clients, the broker-dealer will enter into a selling agreement with the DST sponsor company. This in turn allows the registered representatives to offer their clients investments in the DST property.

It is important to know that just because a broker-dealer has conducted due diligence on a DST property, this does not guarantee that a particular DST offering is safe or guaranteed. Due diligence does not guarantee profits, returns or safety of a particular offering. Investors should be aware that unforeseen problems with DSTs could result in losing some of, or the entirety of, their principal. This is real estate, and there are no guarantees.

Choosing a Securities Representative
Investors will want to work with a securities representative who really understands DST programs. Make time to meet the representative at their place of business. This will provide an opportunity to get a sense of their organizational skills, their support staff, and the overall success of the business. Representatives, who work from home or who have limited support staff, are much more likely to come up short when you need them the most.

Unexpected things can happen, even with the best investments, and you should feel comfortable that your representative and their firm will be there to support you for the entire investment cycle. Unless you reside in a major metropolitan area, you may need to interact with a securities representative who is not local to you. This should not automatically be a disqualifier because many investors successfully conclude DST investments with representatives outside of their area. It is generally better to work with a more highly qualified representative out of your area than someone local who may lack the needed expertise and full credentials to provide comprehensive service to you.

Lessons from Experience

I hold a real estate license, securities license, mortgage broker license and insurance license, and I'm an enrolled agent tax professional. Real estate has been in my blood for my entire business career.

I've learned how valuable a professional with licensing in multiple areas related to DST investing can be when investing in DSTs. Someone who holds only a securities license is absolutely qualified to offer DSTs, but they may not have a complete understanding of how these properties work and the potential benefits and risks.

For Realtors Interested in DSTs

Although DSTs aren't within the purview of realtors' training or licensing, many realtors are eager for more knowledge about this type of investment. They know that the partnership between a residential or commercial real estate agent and an investment adviser who specializes in real estate can be very strong.

Realtors often come into contact with the type of investors that are tired of the hands-on management of being a landlord and are seeking higher cash flows to fund their current or future retirement. However, realtors, like the investor themselves, may be under the impression that capital gains taxes will be exorbitant if the client sells the current property. And though many realtors are aware of 1031 exchanges, many have never heard of DSTs as an investment option.

When realtors become exposed to the mechanics and structuring of a 1031 exchange, they can urge their clients to explore the available tax benefits of selling their investment property. Understanding DSTs can help realtors present a very attractive investment option to their clients, giving clients a compelling reason to consider selling current properties instead of keeping rental units that are no longer satisfying their personal and financial needs.

The Role of a Qualified Intermediary in a 1031 Exchange

In order to execute a successful 1031 exchange, the IRS stipulates that an investor cannot take possession of the proceeds from the sale of their property or they will void the tax benefit of the exchange. So the first step in initiating a 1031 exchange is electing a so-called qualified intermediary (QI), a third-party representative who coordinates items related to the purchase and sale of investment properties.

When you sell an existing property, proceeds from the sale go to the QI, who holds that money in an escrow account. When you purchase a replacement property, the QI delivers the funds to the closing agent and the new property is deeded over to you. Fees charged by a QI for a standard deferred exchange typically fall between $500 and $1,500 depending on the location and number of properties involved in a transaction.

While a qualified intermediary does not provide specific legal or tax advice, they typically offer investors the following services:

- coordinating communications between the investor and their financial advisers to structure a successful exchange

- preparing the required documentation for the sold or relinquished property and the new replacement property

- providing instructions to the escrow agent and documents to complete the exchange

- placing funds in an insured bank account pending the completion of the exchange

- providing documents to transfer the replacement property to the investor and delivering the exchange proceeds (previously held in escrow) at the closing

- holding the indemnification documents of the replacement properties submitted by the investor

- providing a written account of the exchange transactions for the investor's records

- providing a completed form 1099 to both the investor and the IRS, detailing all proceeds and interest earned by exchange funds and paid to the taxpayer

- preparing exchange documentation

- holding relinquished property funds in a trust

- ensuring that the transaction complies with the guidelines outlined in the tax law

Given the number of parties and moving parts involved in a 1031 exchange, investors would be wise to open a segregated 1031 exchange account as soon as a sales contract has been executed on the sale of their property. Establishing that account early on in the process helps the QI in the performance of their duties, from reviewing the transaction to preparing documents and coordinating the actions of those involved. In a pinch—if you're nearing the end of your 45-day replacement property identification period—an experienced QI can set up an exchange account and prepare the necessary documents just days before a closing. But working on such a tight deadline leaves less time for reviewing decisions and processes and is not in your best interest as an investor. What's critical is involving a

QI in the exchange process before you close escrow. Once that has taken place, it's too late to engage their services and complete a successful exchange.

Choosing a QI

Despite increasing regulation across most industries today, QIs are not subject to any federal or state regulation or oversight. Without any licensing or continuing education requirements, it's relatively easy for anyone to get into the business. That lax regulatory environment means that investors themselves are responsible for ensuring that the QI they hire is truly qualified and trustworthy.

A negligent or inexperienced QI could make an error that jeopardizes your 1031 exchange, resulting in a reversal of claimed benefits and leaving you subject to stiff fines. A dishonest QI could cost you far more.

During a 1031 exchange, significant assets are transferred from your escrow account directly to an account managed by your QI. There have been cases in which an unscrupulous QI secretly invested a client's money into questionable and highly speculative investments without their knowledge. Others have stolen funds outright and then disappeared.

Be selective in your choice of a QI and use a professional with impeccable credentials and a long track record of success. Many excellent QIs are affiliated with banks or large title insurance companies. That association with a reputable company is typically a good endorsement of their character, but it shouldn't be the only factor in your decision. Given the complexity of a 1031 exchange and the potential for extremely costly errors, you should also consider the experience of the professional in question. With tens of thousands of dollars on the line, you don't want the new QI in the office overseeing your exchange.

Questions to ask a potential QI:

- How long have you been in business?

- How many exchanges have you completed in the last five years, and what is the aggregate dollar amount of the exchanges in each of these years?

- What percentage of your business is traditional delayed/forward exchanges versus more complex types, like reverse or improvement exchanges?

- How will my funds be held? Are they held in a segregated account or commingled with other exchange monies?

- Where will my funds be held? What kind and how much insurance does the QI firm carry?

Visit the Federation of Exchange Accommodators' website at www.1031.org to find a list of QIs in your area and learn more about their role in your exchange, or ask your financial adviser for a referral.

Important Timing Considerations

One of the most important elements of the 1031 exchange process is completing the transaction within the time frame outlined by the IRS. When you sell and close escrow on your relinquished property, you must exchange that asset with a new property within 180 calendar days. Keep in mind that the allotted time includes holidays and weekends. So if 180 days from closing escrow happens to fall on a Sunday, your exchange must be completed on the previous Friday—that's because it may not be possible to close the sale on a weekend or holiday. There are no extensions granted on that deadline. The IRS is exacting when it comes to this rule, but that still gives you roughly six months to complete your exchange.

For most investors, 180 days is plenty of time to close on a replacement property and complete a 1031 exchange. What can be more challenging is identifying potential replacement properties within 45 days of closing on the property being sold. The IRS gives investors a month and a half to file an identification letter, nominating a number of potential properties they're considering for purchase. That list is final; it cannot be added to once the identification letter is submitted, which means that in order to complete the exchange, investors must purchase at least one of the options proposed.

To avoid any potential complications and reduce stress, investors should identify replacement properties well before the 45-day deadline. In fact, many of our clients are under contract to buy a replacement property the moment they know that they're selling. Once they've closed on the sale of their property, they're closing on the purchase of another.

The IRS is active in its enforcement of the rules surrounding 1031 exchanges, including time requirements. In fact, since 2012, tax authorities have targeted the transactions with increased scrutiny. In addition to auditing individual investors, the tax authority also audits 1031 exchange accommodators. Attempting to bend the 1031 exchange rules, including backdating documents in order to satisfy IRS deadlines, is a criminal offense. Doing so can result in steep fines for investors and federal charges for QIs.

With proper planning and the partnership of a capable intermediary, you can help ensure that your 1031 exchange satisfies both the IRS as well as your tax-planning needs.

Risk in Owning DST Investments

DST properties are composed of real estate, and as such, they come with many of the same risks that all other forms of real estate entail. The discussion that follows is an overview of some potential risks inherent in DST ownership. This is not an exhaustive list, and investors should review the risks section of the offering document for each potential DST property with a qualified registered representative before investing.

Whether you're investing in homes, duplexes, apartment buildings or commercial properties, there is an element of speculation and a high degree of risk. There is no guarantee with real estate investing. Projected cash flow and appreciation may not be achieved, and investors should be able to bear the potential complete loss of an investment. All real estate and DST programs are subject to the risks of increased and ongoing vacancy, tenant bankruptcies, problematic tenants, loss of day-to-day management control, economic downturns, physical damage and liability, unexpected repairs and maintenance, eminent domain, negative rezoning, interest rate fluctuations, and overall valuation fluctuations. The use of leverage in real estate investments may also increase volatility.

What's more, real estate investments and DST properties entail fees related to the acquisition, syndication, ongoing management and eventual disposition of the property. These fees could materially impact the performance of the investment. Likewise, there may be unforeseen tax consequences that come with investing in DSTs. Here's a look at the limitations and risks that investors might encounter.

Limitations

The IRS issued Revenue Ruling 2004–86, allowing a properly structured DST to qualify as a like-kind 1031 exchange replacement property. Within this revenue ruling, the IRS enumerated "seven deadly sins" that placed limitations on what a trustee can do with a DST property:

1. Once the offering is closed, there can be no future contributions of capital to the DST by either current or new co-investors or beneficiaries.

2. The trustee of the DST cannot renegotiate the terms of the existing loans, nor can it borrow any new funds from any other lender or party.

3. The trustee cannot reinvest proceeds from the sale of investment real estate.

4. The trustee is limited to making capital expenditures with respect to the property to those for a normal repair and maintenance, minor nonstructural capital improvements, and those required by law.

5. Any liquid cash held in the DST between distribution dates can only be invested in short-term debt obligations.

6. All cash, other than necessary reserves, must be distributed to the co-investors or beneficiaries on a current basis.

7. The trustee cannot enter into new leases or renegotiate the current leases.

These seven deadly sins can be problematic for 1031 exchange investors, and violating these rules can potentially trigger tax consequences. However, most sponsors have structured the DST with master leases that allow them the flexibility to address some of the issues that the seven deadly sins create. Also, most sponsors typically use long-term financing that can allow a DST property to be sold prior to the need to either pay off or refinance the loan on the property. However, there are no guarantees that a master lease or long-term financing can protect the investor from unforeseen tax consequences.

Fees

All real estate and DST properties entail fees and costs that investors should review and consider carefully with their CPA or attorney and financial adviser prior to making an investment. Fees and costs should be weighed carefully against the potential for tax deferral using a 1031 exchange. All fees and costs are outlined in each private placement memorandum for investors to review and agree to prior to making an investment.

Debt

Some DSTs will have financing, and others will be structured with no debt at all. A DST program that has no debt poses less risk to investors, since there is no possibility of foreclosure. However, since there is no leverage it may hinder annual cash returns and could affect the likelihood of the return of capital at disposition given no increase in "built-in" equity through amortization of in-place debt.

Market and Valuation Fluctuations

Real estate is subject to market cycles, just like any other investment. A piece of property may rise in value, or it may fall. DSTs have the potential to provide great financial returns, but they're not immune to changes in the economy. Such risks include, but are not limited to, the loss of principal, variations in occupancy, illiquidity and changes to the value of the underlying investments.

Inflation

Some DSTs invest in triple-net retail investments. One of the more attractive elements of this type of investment is having long-term leases in place with major tenants. Turnover is typically low, and the corporation often guarantees lease payments. In such a long lease, the lease payments don't increase frequently—perhaps every five years—and they only increase in small amounts. The terms of your lease dictate the yield and cash flow. Yet, this situation can open investors up to inflation risk.

For example, if your retail property has a 10-year lease with a yield of 5%, and five years from now all other comparable properties on the marketplace have leases in place that allow for yields of 7 to 8%, you've lost potential income. The same long-term fixed lease that gives you security and keeps the yield from shifting downward with the market at the same time doesn't allow the yield to shift upward. In this case, it's entirely possible that you won't keep up with inflation.

This risk is most often seen in retail and office properties that lend themselves to longer-term leases. Investors can control this risk by investing in multifamily apartments, student housing and self-storage or smaller retail units. There, rents can be raised or lowered with the market. Of course, if the local marketplace doesn't allow raising rents, you will remain at the same yield level and length of lease. There is much more opportunity to make adjustments with shorter-term leases.

Interest rates
If you're involved in properties with long leases and few increases in lease rates over time, there is a chance that your investment return will not keep up with interest rates in the marketplace.

Illiquidity
Like all real estate investments, DSTs are illiquid. This property cannot be sold or exchanged for cash quickly. Holding DSTs

for five to ten years on average is not uncommon. The holding period could be shorter or longer, depending on market conditions. There is currently no secondary market for DST ownership shares. The industry has no multiple listing services as in simple real estate ownership. However, it is possible to sell your interest back to the sponsor or to another investor in the DST. It's likely these interests will sell at a discount to the purchase price you originally paid.

Management

Investors must be willing to rely on the trustees, the asset manager and the property manager to make property-related decisions. Beneficial owners of the trust possess limited control and rights. The trust will be operated and managed solely by the trustee, and beneficial owners have no right to participate in the management of the trust.

When the property is not managed at an optimal level, return is always affected. Both the property manager and the asset manager manage DSTs, and each plays a different role. A property manager's job is to implement the business plan, increase income and lower expenses. As a result, net operating income should increase over time. An asset manager watches the property as if they owned it themselves, managing the property manager with the same goal of increasing net operating income as much as possible, which increases cash flow and appreciation potential. The asset manager also watches the market for sales opportunities and decides when it's time to sell, reports to investors periodically, and is responsible for keeping investors abreast of what's going on with the property and answering any questions.

Operator risk spikes if the property manager or asset manager aren't doing a good job. While you can't account for all human behavior, you can make a point of only working with highly experienced sponsors who have excellent track records and sterling reputations. Have candid conversations with the people who will be in charge of your investments and determine for yourself whether they have the character and experience to make sound judgments in your best interests.

The risk in investing in DSTs is equivalent to the risk with real estate you presently own, including your own home. The local market can drop, the economy can decline, or a tornado can cut a swath through the town. All of these events will affect the condition, income and expenses, and eventually the sales price of the property.

While no one has a crystal ball, there are ways to proactively mitigate these kinds of risk. It's important that you have a well-diversified portfolio in markets that are growing. And don't underestimate the importance of spending sufficient time doing your due diligence to ensure the property is a good investment.

Remember that past performance doesn't ensure future performance. Property appreciation and projected income are not guaranteed. It is possible to lose equity in a DST investment. Just like any real estate you may purchase, it is important to pick the right property as well as a strong sponsor to mitigate some of these risks.

Navigating real estate risk, operator risk, interest rate risk and liquidity risk can be tricky, but it's easier when you're armed with appropriate experience and expertise. It's essential to have an experienced adviser who can guide you through the process. With the proper understanding of all the variables at play, these risks can be greatly reduced.

Active vs. Passive Property Investors

Before you invest in real estate of any kind, including through a 1031 exchange, you have to ask yourself how involved you're willing, and able, to be in that process. That is, do you want to be an active or passive investor?

Active investors are directly involved in finding, financing and maintaining investment properties. In addition to personally guaranteeing loans to purchase real estate, active investors handle tenant and maintenance issues, manage accounting and tax matters, and closely oversee the sale or refinancing of their properties when appropriate. Managing a traditional rental property can be taxing and time-consuming work, but it also has its benefits. Active investors not only have full control over the selection of their properties but their activity entitles them to a number of potentially significant tax advantages.

Passive investors, as the name suggests, can be less concerned with the day-to-day responsibilities of traditional real estate investing. Many passive investors begin their real estate investment careers in active roles, and as they become older and more risk-averse, they become more interested in real estate as a source of reliable monthly income. Property investments can provide that, as well as a range of estate-planning tools and tax benefits, which—although there are fewer available than with active investing strategies—are still significant.

Investors in a DST have the benefits of both active and passive forms, which makes DSTs an attractive and useful tool for 1031 participants. Investors not only have access to tax benefits and professional management, they have a greater degree of control over the selection of properties than they would with other passive investment forms, like real estate mutual funds or investment trusts.

With a DST, the investment is structured around a business plan driven by an active professional real estate manager. This often results in an investment that provides individual property investors, even active ones, with superior cash flow than they could produce on their own. In fact, access to that expert management—both the rewards it provides and the potential headaches it can relieve—is what makes DSTs such attractive choices for active investors interested in using a 1031 exchange to transition into a passive role. For many, it means more money and less time spent dealing with tenants, toilets and trash.

Given their structure, DSTs offer investors a number of advantages:

- Simplicity. Completing a 1031 exchange can be complicated, from selling a rental home to working with a qualified intermediary and selecting the proper replacement property. With a DST, once that up-front legwork is complete, the management and administration of the investment is taken care of. Investors simply have to wait for funds to hit their bank account each month.

- Diversity. DSTs invest in different kinds of properties—from residential and retail to commercial and industrial—all across the country, allowing investors to diversify their real estate portfolios beyond local markets.

- Closing speed. Investors can close on a DST opportunity within three to five business days of receiving a subscription agreement and associated documents from the DST sponsor. For 1031 exchange participants feeling the pressure of identifying a replacement property within the required 45-day window, the speed of that closing process can be a welcome feature.

- Quality. DSTs provide individual investors with access to large-scale, institutional-grade real estate projects that are otherwise unavailable to them. With a typical minimum investment of $100,000, DSTs allow investors to purchase ownership interest in multi million-dollar projects, which have a greater potential for return than they would find in a condo, single-family home or multi-unit rental.

The Responsibility of Sponsors

A DST is established and overseen by a person or business entity known as a sponsor. A sponsor typically acquires one or more institutional-grade properties of a similar type, packages them into a DST legal structure, and offers them to accredited investors through a securities professional. While the investors are the actual owners of the properties, the sponsor manages the DST on their behalf in pursuit of the highest financial benefit. Sponsors typically employ both a property manager and asset management team. Asset managers design and administer the business plan for the property, while the property manager is responsible for implementing it.

One of the greatest values a sponsor brings to a DST is their experience in the selection of property. Rather than investing on a hunch or a feeling, sponsors select markets and properties that they believe will be profitable, using objective criteria developed over many years. Their relationships with private sellers often allow them to acquire off-market property well below its appraised value.

Sponsors tend to specialize in specific sectors and types of real estate; one might focus on retail, another on multifamily apartments and another on student housing. This specialization and resulting expertise in one segment of real estate investing is the key to generating healthy, consistent returns.

How Sponsors Maximize Return

A sponsor's ability to generate positive returns is based on increasing the net operating income of a property over the life of the DST. Net operating income is calculated as total income minus total expenses (excluding loan payments). Actions that either increase income or reduce expenses positively impact net operating income and provide more return for the investors. Sponsors manage both of those factors aggressively and in a number of ways.

In multifamily apartments, sponsors frequently survey the rental market, adjusting the rates for both new leases and renewals. They seek out additional sources of income from tenants, including pet fees, parking, storage and features such as valet trash pickup or utility charge-backs. Sponsors carefully curate and enhance the image of the property and its facilities through new amenities and services—improvements that allow them to increase the lease rate while retaining current clients and attracting prospective ones.

The sponsor of a DST works to increase net operating income until it becomes advantageous to sell the underlying property.

A DST, like any rental real estate opportunity, is a long-term investment. The life of a DST is typically between 5 to 10 years, though depending on local market conditions, some properties are held for longer. However, the business plan requires the asset manager to continually review the likelihood of a successful sale beginning with the third year of ownership.

When a DST's asset manager makes the decision to sell a property, investors receive their pro rata share of the proceeds and are free to make new investment decisions. As an investor, you may choose to cash out and pay taxes on any capital gains due. You can also perform another 1031 exchange, deferring taxes through the purchase of another like-kind investment property, including another DST.

Unlocking the Equity in a Rental Property
One of the unique benefits of a DST is that it allows active property investors to unlock the equity in their rental properties. In doing so, the DST can help investors generate more recurring income while providing them with more free time to enjoy it.

Many of the most successful real estate investors over the last two decades are those who invested in the booming housing market. With a rapidly growing economy and increased housing demand, many homeowners have seen their properties dramatically increase in value. With the increase in value came a higher amount of equity retained in the investment. While this appreciation in value is a benefit for the investor, the challenge is that the equity gain in the investment is not being put to work.

Consider this hypothetical example. Bob and Mary bought a Bay Area home in the early 1980s for a whopping $125,000 with a $25,000 down payment. Since the time of their purchase, Bob and Mary have moved into a new home with their growing family and are now renting out their first house to tenants. As a younger couple, they had the time and energy to manage both the upkeep on the home and the various tenants who cycled through the property. Now that they're approaching retirement, they're no longer interested in the responsibility of being a landlord.

Their first home is now worth $1,400,000, with roughly $1,300,000 in equity after closing costs. The rent they received from the property provides about $20,000 in annual pretax cash flow after expenses. However, they have exhausted the allowed depreciation benefits of the property, meaning they now have less after-tax income.

The couple decides to sell their rental property and complete a 1031 exchange to move their proceeds into a small portfolio of DST properties, which includes single-tenant retail properties and a multifamily asset. They now own a diversified portfolio of institutional-grade real estate and none of the responsibility they shouldered as landlords. What's more, they are utilizing the equity from their former investment property and realizing an average 5 to 7% annualized cash flow, which delivers about $75,000 in annual income that is mostly tax-sheltered.

For active real estate investors interested in maintaining a good, recurring source of income without the hassle and headaches of being property manager, a DST could be just the answer they're looking for.

Who Should Invest in a DST?

DSTs are available to accredited investors only (with limited exceptions, see Rule 506 of Regulation D). An accredited investor is an individual or an entity—including trusts, brokers, banks and insurance companies—that can invest in securities that are not registered with the SEC. Companies might offer securities to accredited investors to avoid the cost of regulatory filings when raising capital. The SEC deems accredited individuals and entities financially sophisticated enough to not require the protections offered by regulatory disclosure filings.

To become an accredited investor, one must meet a number of requirements surrounding income, net worth, asset size, governance status, or professional experience. A person or entity must meet the following requirements:

- Income. The investor must have had an annual income of $200,000 for individuals or $300,000 for couples for the last two years. Additionally, they must expect to earn the same income or higher in the current year. An individual must have earned income above these thresholds either alone or with a spouse—but not a mix—over three years. In other words, the income test cannot be met with two years of joint income and one year of individual income. However, there is an exception to this rule if a person gets married within the period of conducting this test.

- Net worth. Investors may be accredited if they have a net worth exceeding $1 million, either individually or jointly with a spouse, excluding the value of a primary residence.

- Professional experience. You may be an accredited investor if you are a general partner, executive officer or director for the issuer of unregistered securities. Additionally, in 2016, the U.S. Congress modified the definition of an accredited investor to include registered brokers and investment advisers. If a person can demonstrate sufficient education or job experience showing professional knowledge of unregistered securities, they may be considered an accredited investor.

Private business development companies with assets over $5 million may be accredited investors. However, organizations cannot be formed for the purpose of purchasing specific securities. Entities comprising accredited investors are themselves accredited investors.

Investors over age 50 are often great candidates for DST investing, especially if they already hold investment properties. Certainly, younger clients can invest in DSTs as well. Investors over 50 have frequently already been active in locating, purchasing and managing investment properties. Yet, as they enter their 50s, they may be less interested in managing these properties as they wrap up work and look toward retirement. This is where a DST can be particularly useful as it offers a way to stay invested in real estate without managing it personally.

As investors reach their 60s and retirement is upon them, there is an added incentive to use DSTs to simplify their lives so they can enjoy the fruits of their labor. At this time, investors often need cash flow to fund their retirements. This cash flow potential, even more so than appreciation, is the primary consideration in their real estate investments. For that reason, DSTs become strategically important.

Investors in their 70s and beyond are well into enjoying their retirement. The thought of any more late-night phone calls is beyond irritating, they're done fixing toilets! There still is time left for thoughtful investing, and the estate planning aspects of 1031 exchanges into DSTs are very appealing.

DSTs Aren't for Everyone

For all of the advantages DSTs offer, they aren't always the right fit for investors.

First off, it's important to note that DST 1031 properties are real estate, and like all other types of real estate, they are inherently illiquid. You are not buying shares of stock listed on a public exchange that you can sell in 10 seconds by logging into your online brokerage account. This is a fractional beneficial interest in a trust that owns a large piece of illiquid real estate. As such, investors should be willing and able to hold their investments in the DST 1031 property for the full life of the program, which could last for 7 to 10 years or even longer.

That being said, it is possible for investors to sell DST interest in a property before its full cycle event. Typically, if an investor wants to sell his or her interest in a DST property, the sponsor will send a letter to all of the other DST investors in the property, notifying them that a fellow investor wants to exit their interest in the property. That said, there is no guarantee that an investor will be able to find another investor who wants to buy the DST interest or that they will be able to agree on a price.

Also, there is an inherent loss of control that comes with the hands-off nature of DSTs. For investors who enjoy managing properties themselves, this can be a negative instead of a positive. These investors generally like control of their properties and enjoy managing them and obtaining the best possible return.

Simply being an accredited investor does not mean that DSTs are automatically right for you. Though a potential investor may meet the SEC's criteria on paper, their financial adviser must take the investor's entire portfolio into consideration to determine whether an investment is suitable. For example, if a client's entire portfolio is invested in real estate and completely without diversification, the adviser is tasked with informing the potential investor that a sound portfolio strategy would be to cash out some real estate proceeds and invest in stocks, bonds and mutual funds. Liquidity and a balanced portfolio are prudent, and diversification is the key.

Other qualified accredited investors may meet the income requirements but have a weak cash position. Putting their money into an illiquid investment for 5 to 10 years or longer may not be prudent. Rather, it may be wise for them to perform a partial exchange, pay the taxes on the proceeds, and give themselves a cash buffer.

Who's Who: The Different Players

In this chapter, I will provide an overview of the sponsors who provide Delaware statutory trust (DST) offerings. The number of firms offering securitized real estate peaked in 2006 and dramatically declined during the 2008 recession, which forced many of the less capitalized firms to close. As real estate values have increased recently (I'm writing this in December 2017) some sponsors have reentered the market. However, increased scrutiny by lenders and broker-dealers has limited the entry of new sponsors, as all new sponsors are required to meet increasingly strenuous standards. Today, there are around 30 sponsors. A partial list and discussion of sponsoring firms follows later in this chapter.

What is a DST sponsor? A DST sponsor has much in common with other firms that locate and manage investment real estate on behalf of investors. They work closely with the real estate brokerage community to find attractively priced offerings that are suitable for investors, typically off-market properties that are not being publicly marketed. They also have close relationships with multiple loan providers who can provide optimum financing to allow investors to reap maximum income from their investments. They tend to specialize in specific asset classes and geographical areas, and they possess sufficient infrastructure to maintain ongoing investor and lender reporting.

DST sponsors are different from traditional real estate investment managers in a few ways. They are responsible for obtaining loans, they are solely responsible to the lender for any loan guarantees, and they must meet balance sheet requirements to support multiple loans. They typically take ownership of their properties prior to exposing them to investors, thereby taking on additional capital risk. If a sponsor's offerings are not fully subscribed, they are left with any unsold interests, and the sponsor must leave capital tied up until the asset is sold.

Sponsors' offerings are sold through licensed securities brokers, who impose added levels of due diligence and ongoing performance scrutiny. Their offerings are approved for sale to investors subject to third-party due diligence reports that summarize the offering structure, fees and prior performance of the sponsor, among other items.

Due primarily to the requirement of capital risk and heightened scrutiny by the broker-dealer community, relatively few real estate management firms participate in sponsoring DST offerings.

The players as of June 2018 taken from their respective Websites are as follows:

AEI was founded in 1970. It is one of the country's oldest sponsors of net leased real estate investment programs, as well as a leader in the 1031 property exchange industry. The firm has been completing successful securitized 1031 exchanges on behalf of investors since 1992. As a pioneer in this business, AEI was the first sponsor to receive a favorable private letter ruling with regard to its offering structure in 2003. Currently, AEI focuses on properties with no debt and designs its program with a 10-year hold term in mind. By having projects with no debt, the company reduces risk, since there is no possibility of foreclosure. Over the past 40 years, AEI has sponsored 126 net leased real estate programs, representing the investment capital from more than 20,000 investors nationwide and acquiring more than 383 properties.

Black Creek Group, out of Denver, has been operating since the early 1990s and has executed more than $17.7 billion in real estate transactions through hundreds of separate closings. It has sponsored 18 investment platforms, including 13 institutional and five retail funds; owned and operated more than 1,300 office, industrial, retail and multifamily properties across North America; and developed more than $3 billion in properties across North America. Black Creek is one of Walmart's global development partners, having built 68 stores, covering approximately 5 million square feet, and having developed or acquired more than 120 retail properties, totaling approximately 20 million square feet across North America.

Bluerock is a New York City–based private equity real estate investment firm founded in 2010. It is a full-service national investment firm, offering a mix of public and private institutional investments, with both short- and long-term goals, to real estate investors. Bluerock's senior management team has an average of over 25 years of investing experience and has acquired or developed more than 85 real estate properties. These properties include 48 apartment complexes totaling more than 10,000 apartment units, representing approximately 14 million combined square feet across 14 states and more than $2 billion in acquisition value. The firm currently has more than $2.3 billion of real estate assets under management, the majority of which are apartment communities in sought-after growth areas throughout the United States.

Bourne Financial Group is headquartered in Winter Park, Florida, and was founded in 2014 by Robert A. Bourne and R. Kyle Bourne. Bourne Financial is a real estate investment company, specializing in senior housing development, acquisitions and asset management. Its leadership team has over 130 years of collective experience investing in health-care real estate, specifically senior housing and medical office buildings, as well as extensive experience in hospitality, retail, restaurant and other real estate sectors. Its principals have helped create or acquire over $30 billion in assets across many real estate sectors, including $6 billion in senior housing and medical office assets in the United States, spanning several market cycles. Bourne's goal is to create a series of health-care investment products for its investors that span the risk-return spectrum. Its strategy is to form strategic alliances with experienced operators and developers in the industry to build or acquire senior housing communities. Bourne's portfolio currently consists of 13 senior housing communities across the United States that are either open or under construction.

Cantor Fitzgerald is one of the newest sponsors to enter the DST market. It is also one of the oldest companies to be participating in the space. Founded in 1945 in New York, Cantor Fitzgerald has established itself as one of the dominant global financial service firms, with significant real estate, capital markets, research and investment experience. The company has a significant presence across the world, with more than 10,000 employees in over 150 offices across 22 countries. As a company, it conducts more than $180 trillion worth of financial transactions annually and has recently invested more than $600 million to establish a multidisciplinary real estate platform with the capability of spanning the investment cycle, including acquisitions, financing, property management, leasing and investment cells. Boasting an investment-grade credit rating by both Standard & Poor's and Fitch Ratings, Cantor Fitzgerald is well positioned to become a dominant force in the DST marketplace.

Capital Square 1031 is a national real estate investment and management company that sponsors institutional-quality real estate exchange programs that qualify for tax deferral under section 1031 of the Internal Revenue Code. The firm uses the

DST structure to make quality real estate investments available to a larger number of investors. Capital Square 1031 was founded in 2012 and has sponsored 35 DST programs to date. None of the DST programs have gone full cycle yet. Capital Square 1031 focuses on acquiring stable multifamily apartment communities and long-term triple-net leased medical properties across the nation. The apartment communities are in well-established neighborhoods surrounded by centers of employment and numerous recreational opportunities. The medical properties are leased by investment-grade tenants on a triple-net, long-term basis with regular rental increases, making for a predictable and increasing income stream from a recession-resistant investment in which the tenant pays virtually all of the operating expenses. The goal is to provide investors with predictable cash flow and the potential for capital appreciation from stable replacement properties that qualify for tax deferral under section 1031.

CORE Pacific Advisors is an investment advisory firm with expertise in commercial real estate and real estate-related investments. It is located in Newport Beach, California, and is an affiliate of CORE Retail Holdings Management. CORE Pacific Advisors is focused on creating and implementing client-focused commercial real estate strategies that provide superior income, capital preservation and growth potential, all delivered with the highest level of integrity, communication and service. With decades of experience in buying, managing and successfully selling commercial real estate in a variety of market conditions, the team concentrates on identifying institutional-quality investments with the potential to outperform the market while at the same time managing risk. At CORE, real estate is a business built on relationships, including those with sellers, brokers, service providers, buyers, and most importantly investors. Over the years, CORE has developed strong relationships throughout the commercial real estate community and earned the trust of thousands of investors nationwide.

Everest Properties is a privately held, diversified real estate investment firm. Everest specializes in the acquisition, recapitalization and asset management of real estate, with significant experience investing in and managing real estate investment trusts, tenancy-in-common, limited liability companies, limited partnerships and DST real estate investment entities. Everest seeks to acquire and finance assets that it believes have a disproportionately high potential investment return compared with the investment risk. It joins its institutional and individual partners and invests its own capital, often owning a substantial majority of the equity of projects within its portfolio. Everest was founded in 1994 and has invested funds in excess of $200 million in more than 650 limited partnerships, providing liquidity for an otherwise illiquid asset class. It is located in Pasadena, California.

Exchange Right is based in Pasadena, California, and initiated its syndication of 1031 DST offerings in 2012. The firm currently has more than 3,200,000 square feet of assets under management, valued at approximately $550 million. Its 195 properties are located throughout 27 states and are structured to provide long-term, stable income and asset preservation for accredited 1031 investors. Until recently, Exchange Right exclusively focused on net leased retail assets with investment-grade corporate tenants operating in the necessity retail space, like Walgreens or CVS pharmacies.

Four Springs Capital Trust is a multifaceted real estate company that was founded in 2012 and is based in Lake Como, New Jersey. The firm offers both real estate investment trusts and DST investments focused on net leased single-tenant retail, medical office and industrial warehouse assets. Four Springs targets triple-net and double-net leased properties that have lease terms greater than 10 years and investment-grade tenants. They will, however, consider private companies with strong balance sheets and income history. With a national footprint, Four Springs separates itself from other sponsors by pursuing build-to-suit properties that are acquired directly from developers. Its goal is to mitigate risk from economic downturns in local markets by diversifying its DST offerings. It seeks to accomplish this by acquiring a greater amount of small single-tenant properties, as opposed to a small amount of large multi-tenant properties.

Inland Private Capital Corporation was originally founded in 1969 in Oak Brook, Illinois. The firm has sponsored over 704 programs across 43 states, including seven real estate investment trusts, 687 private placements and 10 limited partnerships. With over $10.5 billion in completed transactions and more than 490,000 investors, Inland is one of the most experienced sponsors in the market, engaging in all facets of real estate, including property management, leasing, marketing, acquisition, disposition, development, redevelopment, renovation, instruction, and finance. Inland Real Estate's fully integrated group of legally and financially independent companies has Inland Private Capital Corporation as the specific sponsor of its 1031 DST properties. One of Inland's strengths is its alignment with investors through direct investment of $113 million into its own programs. Not only is it one of the most dominant DST sponsors in the market but, as demonstrated by the above figures, Inland is one of the largest investment, commercial real estate and financial institutions in the country.

KB Exchange Trust is owned by Kingsbarn Realty Capital, a real estate private equity firm focused on providing structured real estate investments to high-net-worth individuals, family trusts, foundations and institutional investors. Kingsbarn Realty Capital acquires commercial real estate assets throughout the

United States. It offers both direct and indirect real estate investments and provides its clients with the opportunity to invest in various structured real estate private placements. Kingsbarn's management team has extensive experience developing, managing and sponsoring a diverse array of stabilized core properties and income-driven investment funds. KB Exchange Trust acquires single-tenant properties leased to health-care-related companies on long-term leases. These companies are generally highly regarded, publicly traded companies with revenues exceeding $1 billion annually. The Delaware statutory trust ownership structure makes these investments ideal for investors who are in a 1031 exchange. The investment amount is flexible, starting at $100,000, which is also beneficial to 1031 exchange investors who are trying to invest an amount equivalent to their down-leg exchange, the initial property sale.

Livingston Street Capital is a boutique commercial real estate private equity firm focused on health-care, multifamily and mission-critical real estate. Its goal is to protect and enhance investment capital throughout multiple economic cycles, and its team has completed over $1.1 billion in acquisitions across the United States. It currently manages a national portfolio of real estate across 18 states. Livingston Street Capital's strategy is to focus on real estate investments that serve the essential needs of individuals and corporations. Its corporate headquarters is in Radnor, Pennsylvania.

Madison Realty, with offices in Denver and Pasadena, California, was founded over 20 years ago and is a private real estate firm with expertise in acquiring income-producing real estate. Each member of its senior executive team has 30-plus years of individual experience. It has acquired and managed over $6 billion of U.S. real estate in over 30 states. Madison focuses on purchasing properties below market value to provide a margin of error when it comes to returning principal. It upgrades or expands properties to add value and capital appreciation.

Moody National Realty is the subsidiary of Moody National Companies that acquires and syndicates real estate offerings across the United States. It is an all-encompassing real estate company operating subsidiary companies focused on mortgage lending, development, management, syndication, title, and insurance. Moody National Companies was formed in 1996 and is headquartered in Houston. Moody National Realty has been involved in the acquisition and syndication of real estate since its inception, with a total of 46 privately offered real estate programs funded by more than 1,250 investors and producing a total capitalization of approximately $1.4 billion. In addition, Moody National Realty specializes in hospitality assets throughout the United States and has acquired more than 65 class A hotel properties. Its primary focus for its DST platform is the syndication of triple-net retail and multifamily properties. Moody targets well maintained class A assets that are located along the East and West coasts as well in the Sun Belt region. Its investment criteria includes a focus on major metropolitan population centers located in states that are ranked within the top quartile of US population growth.

Nelson Brothers Professional Real Estate started operations in 2007 and has acquired and managed over $240 million in assets through the acquisition of 19 student-housing properties and three assisted-living properties across 10 states. Nelson Brothers focuses on targeted growth opportunities and value-added investments for its clients through capital improvements, cost efficiency and revenue maximization. Its entities include Nelson Brothers Professional Real Estate and Nelson Brothers Property Management. Its strategy is to focus on assets that cater to growing demands, particularly niche industries, such as assisted living or collegiate housing, that it believes to be stable and less correlated to market fluctuations.

Further, both target demographics, college students and the elderly, are desirable demographics. Nelson Brothers Properties is located in Aliso Viejo, California. In mid-2018 this company split into two companies: NB Private Capital and Nelson Partners Student Housing.

Net Lease Capital Advisors was formed in 1996 and is based in Nashua, New Hampshire. Since its inception, it has closed over $9 billion worth of real estate transactions. Net Lease Capital Advisors focuses exclusively on single-tenant, triple-net properties and has predominately syndicated highly leveraged, zero cash flow DST offerings. The properties it pursues tend to be larger in scale, with credit tenants rated BBB or better, including government tenants and national company headquarters. Its acquisition criteria include preferred lease terms in the 15- to 20-year range, with transaction size ranging anywhere from $20 million to more than $500 million. One of the more experienced DST sponsors, Net Lease Capital Advisors has a platform that primarily addresses the niche market of investors looking for high-debt investments with little or no income and the objective of avoiding taxes. It has fully funded nine DST offerings to date, and one has gone full cycle. Its first completed program was the Sun Microsystems headquarters property, which it re-tenanted upon lease expiration, refinancing the debt to create a positive return for investors. Facebook's corporate headquarters are currently in this building, which is located in East Palo Alto, California.

NexPoint, an affiliate of Highland Capital Management, is an independently owned investment firm with over 20 years of experience in a broad range of products for both retail and institutional investors. It boasts a rapidly growing team of over 180 employees based around the world. NexPoint is headquartered in Dallas, with a network of offices in New York City, São Paulo, Singapore and Seoul, South Korea. Its diversified client base includes pension plans, foundations and endowments, corporations, financial institutions, governments, and high-net worth individuals. Highland's focus is on delivering alpha and providing value to investors by offering unique products, pursuing new opportunities, and passionately protecting investors' capital.

Passco Companies was founded in 1998 and is headquartered in Irvine, California. Passco is a nationally recognized real estate investment firm that specializes in the acquisition, development and management of multifamily and commercial properties throughout the United States. With assets spanning 20 states, it has surpassed $3 billion in acquisitions and is approaching $2 billion of assets under management, with more than 5,000 investors worldwide. The Passco management team averages 34 years of real estate experience and has collectively acquired more than $30 billion of investment real estate projects across the country. Passco seeks to acquire primarily core and value-added multifamily properties with 200 or more units, as well as retail properties and regional shopping centers in California, Washington, Arizona, Nevada, and Texas. In recent years Passco has focused exclusively on multifamily properties for its DST offerings.

Rance King Properties, known as RK Properties, is a Delaware corporation that has specialized in multifamily investment since 1976. Rance King Securities Corporation is a California corporation that was formed in 1984 and acts as the placement agent for investment products sponsored by RK Properties. Both RK Properties and Rance King Securities Corporation are owned by William Rance King, Jr., who is both a registered Financial Industry Regulatory Authority principal and a multistate licensed real estate broker. Having exclusively been in the apartment investment business since 1976, RK Properties finds itself without many peers. The key to its success is that it created a specialized market niche and filled it well for decades. When it first started buying apartment buildings, in the mid 1970s, friends and business associates who saw the rewards often said, "Please count me in." Today, RK Properties is still working with the same philosophy and many of the same supporters. It looks for something special where it knows it can add value—property that will be worthy of both pride and profit. By now, its investor base has grown to more than 3,500 clients.

Real Estate Value Advisors, otherwise known as REVA, is based in Richmond, Virginia, and was formed in 2005 by a team of seasoned real estate professionals with more than 50 years of experience and $12 billion in transactions, including 12 DSTs. With more than a decade of history and nearly $400 million in sponsored transactions, REVA is one of a few sponsors of fractional real estate offerings to weather the 2008 storm and expand its offerings. REVA predominantly focuses on office properties. In addition to syndications for 1031 exchange and cash investments in the DST structure, it also sponsors the REVA Catalyst Fund, which requires office properties with value-added characteristics where there is a need for capital infusion, repositioning or refinancing.

Smartstop Asset Management is a diversified real estate company focused on self-storage assets, along with student and senior housing. The company has managed portfolios that currently include more than 68,000 self-storage units and approximately 7.9 million rentable square feet, and it has approximately $1.3 billion in real estate assets under management. It is an asset manager of 409 self-storage facilities located throughout the United States and Toronto. Smartstop is in Ladera Ranch, California, and has been a leader in self-storage, securitized real estate offerings. In 2017, it entered the student housing and senior housing markets utilizing the 1031 exchange.

Starboard Realty Advisors, headquartered in Irvine, California, is a privately held, fully integrated real estate firm that has more than 35 years of hands-on, cycle-tested experience in acquiring, developing, leasing, repositioning, managing, financing, and disposing of real estate. Starboard acquires primarily multi-tenant retail shopping centers and land for retail development. It offers commercial real estate investment opportunities to accredited investors, family offices and institutional partners in a joint venture, partnership or Delaware statutory trust structure. It acquires and operates properties that have some or all of these attributes: current rents are below market, moderate vacancy, acquired at below replacement costs, developable pads, or moderate renovations needed. It nurtures a service culture by recruiting and retaining like-minded staff. Starboard is recognized in the industry for offering quality real estate investments that meet the objectives of its clients and providing unparalleled communications, reporting and investor service.

In today's highly competitive market, commercial property professionals always look for ways to enhance their value to customers. Luckily, among the greatest tools for attaining this value-add could be the well-known section 1031 tax-deferred exchange. Nearly all industry pros are knowledgeable about the most commonly accepted benefit of a 1031 exchange: The tax, which otherwise would be expected, is deferred. Yet many people have started to understand that exchanging is a powerful tool that can accomplish an assortment of investment objectives beyond lowering the instant tax bill. A particularly intriguing aspect of executing a market plan is its own wealth-building capacity.

People in the financial services industry understand the ramifications of compounding. For instance, an investor who begins funding an individual retirement account at age 20 versus 40 results in a dramatically different retirement balance at age 59 1/2. The easiest of examples is the "double the penny" example, which highlights the sometimes-surprising benefits of compounding. A penny doubled every day for a month is worth only two pennies on day two, but on day 31, it is worth $64 million. Compounding and time can indeed produce impressive investment developments. Potentially the most effective advantage of a 1031 exchange, the compounding impact, is also the most overlooked. The key to receiving the top-compounding result is keeping all the cash working for the investor—not only today but also in the future. In a 1031 exchange, the amount of tax that otherwise would be paid to Uncle Sam is reinvested. The projected future value of the compounded yield on the tax has the potential to get quite substantial over time.

Many real estate investors also add leverage, which considerably amplifies the compounding impact. By way of illustration, consider an investor who sold a $1 million property with a $200,000 basis in 1988. Without utilizing an exchange, the profit on the sale would have been $800,000, with roughly $200,000 due in taxes. After paying the taxes, there would have been approximately $800,000 in after-tax cash to reinvest. However, the investor exchanged the property and purchased a $1 million income-producing replacement property that had been 85% occupied. He put $200,000 down, or exactly the same amount he would have had with no exchange. Two years later, after making mandatory direction adjustments, he increased the property's occupancy to 94% and sold it for $1.4 million. The $200,000 he put down on the property added to the $400,000 he made equals $600,000.

The investor then did a new 1031 exchange and put the $600,000 in profit down on a $2 million income property, which had been undermanaged and was at 83% occupancy. Three years later, after attaining 92% occupancy in the property, the investor sold it for $2.6 million. With the $600,000 he'd put down and the $600,000 he made on the purchase, after only five years that the $200,000 tax, which had been deferred, has climbed to $1.2 million. Alternatively, without the exchange strategy, the investor would have had no additional advantage from his investments because the first $200,000 would have been used to pay the tax.

Compounding mixed with leverage can create wealth very fast. Over a 12-year interval, this investor did five exchanges and turned the money he otherwise would not have had ($200,000) into $4.8 million. Many investors have developed trade strategies that have allowed them to go from a modest net value to a very high net worth in a 10- to 20-year time frame. Clearly, these real-life cases are achieved more easily when property is in an up cycle, but that doesn't negate the potential advantages of using a 1031 exchange plan and holding property during downward cycles. Since there are no restrictions about the number of trades a taxpayer can finish, this strategy may be used throughout the taxpayer's whole lifetime. Although some investors eventually sell property that is acquired via an exchange and pay the tax, it's very common to never cash out and make the investments a part of the client's estate. At that stage, the estate receives a stepped-up basis and the tax disappears.

Naturally, there are additional investment goals that may be accomplished by utilizing the 1031 tax-deferral tool. Some of the most desirable goals include the ability to relocate an investment or sell property in one place and buy another property in a more desirable place. Another advantage is the capability to convert non-cash-flow property into income-producing property by selling undeveloped property and buying income-producing property. Lastly, many taxpayers want to simplify their investments by eliminating headaches. For instance, an investor can sell an apartment complex and buy an office building using one tenant that occupies the space on a triple-net lease basis. While these additional investment strategies are important to particular investment objectives, the one aim of the 1031 market that applies to all customers is the compounding effect of this deferred tax. If commercial real estate professionals can prompt customers to look beyond the instant tax deferral and educate them about the wealth-building capability of a long-term 1031 market strategy, they could actively assist their clients in benefiting from the compounding impact. Knowing the full advantage of this tool can provide commercial property professionals a plan they can use in any market—up or down.

The average investment term of a DST is 5 to 10 years. The sponsors make the decision to sell when the market for a sale is advantageous. When the property is sold, the investor has a decision to make. The proceeds of the sale can be cashed out, the capital gains tax paid, and the net cash out used in any manner the investor wishes—or the proceeds can be reinvested by performing another 1031 exchange. The replacement properties purchased can be DSTs or any other real estate considered like-kind by the IRS.

When an investor chooses to move their proceeds into another 1031 exchange, all of the benefits of the original exchange are compounded. The old capital gains tax that was deferred in the original exchange remains deferred, and the potential tax on the capital gains from the sale of the DST is also deferred.

To illustrate the compounding power of sequential 1031 exchanges, let's look at an example: Say you bought a duplex in 2005 for $1 million, with $500,000 cash and a $500,000 loan. Today, the duplex is worth $1,950,000, and you're ready to sell.

You sell the duplex for $1,967,000, and you have $1,420,000 in proceeds after the cost of the sale. Using a 1031 exchange, you avoid approximately $147,000 in capital gains tax, assuming a 35% total capital gains tax rate. Next, you reinvest the proceeds of the sale into one DST or multiple DSTs to add diversity and safety to your portfolio. With the new DST, the buyer has a 50% loan-to-value ratio, allowing you to purchase $2,841,000 in property value.

After seven and a half years, the DST plan sponsor decides to sell your investment, and the sale price is $3,296,000. You invested $1,420,000 equity in the properties and received $1,958,000 after the sale. To calculate your gain, add your original basis in the duplex, $1 million, to the amount of additional property you bought when you invested in the DST, $1,011,000. Your new basis is $2,011,000, and your total capital gain now is $1,284,000. If you decide to take the proceeds and cash out, your capital gains tax will be approximately $450,000. Instead, say you reinvest all the proceeds into another DST or multiple DSTs. The new DST has a 50% loan-to-value ratio, so you now own $3,916,000 worth of property in your new DST.

Again, you hold the DST and receive cash flow and tax benefits over the years of ownership. Now, let's say that just before your last DST is sold, you pass away at the age of 80-years old, leaving your property to your heirs. The property sells a few months later for a little above $4,500,000, more than quadruple your original investment of $500,000 in the duplex 25 years ago. Your heirs inherit the $2,686,000 proceeds from the sale at a stepped-up basis and owe no capital gains tax on the sale. You accumulated a $1.9 million gain over the 25 years of real estate ownership, and if you had lived and cashed out the property, you would have paid $668,000 in capital gains taxes upon the sale. By using the 1031 exchange, it helped you get more income every year from your investments and provide your heirs with a sizable inheritance. You saved a whopping $668,000 that would have been paid to the government through capital gains taxes.

Even if we assume that your rate of return remains roughly constant. The value of the investment portfolio grows, which increases your cash flow and your overall profit from appreciation. You will live a progressively better lifestyle as you age and eliminate the government from your profits.

Below I'm going to show you a hypothetical timeline for two different investors who bought and sold properties over a 35-year span. The investor in each scenario starts with $50,000 and buys the same property worth $250,000. Each has the same growth of 5% equity growth each year. Later, both reinvest their profits as a 30% down payment on their next real estate purchase but end up with very different amounts due to the taxes. For simplicity, we're not including closing costs, depreciation, loan pay down, cash flow, and other obvious sources of income and expenses in this diagram.

Investor 1

Years	Purchase Price	Sold For	Profit	Equity to Reinvest (1031 Used)
1 to 5	$250,000.00	$319,070.39	$69,070.39	$119,070.39
6 to 10	$595,351.95	$759,836.72	$164,484.77	$283,555.16
11 to15	$1,417,775.79	$1,809,481.10	$391,705.31	$675,260.47
16 to 20	$3,376,302.35	$4,309,112.44	$932,810.09	$1,608,070.56
21 to 25	$8,040,352.79	$10,261,754.02	$2,221,401.23	$3,829,471.79

After five years, Investor 1 sold her property for $319,070.39. She chose to purchase her next property through a 1031 exchange. She was able to use the entire profit and the equity she built to put a 30% down payment on her next deal. The investor continued to make 1031 exchanges every five years for 25 years with no tax due because of the continual use of the 1031 exchange.

Now let's take a look at Investor 2, who chose not to use a 1031 exchange.

Investor 2

Years	Purchase Price	Sold For	Profit	Equity to Reinvest (15% Tax Paid
1 to 5	$250,000.00	$319,070.39	$69,070.39	$108,709.83
6 to 10	$543,549.16	$693,721.77	$150,172.61	$236,356.55
11 to 15	$1,181,782.76	$1,508,287.54	$326,504.79	$513,885.62
16 to 20	$2,569,428.10	$3,279,313.71	$709,885.61	$1,117,288.39
21 to 25	$5,586,441.95	$7,129,972.86	$1,543,430.91	$2,429,204.66

Investors 2 did not use a 1031 exchange. He also made a sale and new property purchase every 5 years, and after 25 years, Investor 2 ended up with just under $2.5 million. While still a respectable sum of money, notice that he trails Investor 1 by over $1,000,000! This is because Investor 1 was able to put the government's money to work, helping her build greater wealth.

Glossary of 1031 Exchange Terms

1031 exchange

The sale or disposition of real estate or personal property (re-linquished property) and the acquisition of like-kind real estate or personal property (replacement property) structured as a tax-deferred, like-kind exchange transaction pursuant to section 1031 of the internal revenue code and section 1.1031 of the treasury regulations in order to defer federal, and in most cases state, capital gain and depreciation recapture taxes.

Accelerated cost recovery system (ACRS)

A depreciation method used for most property placed into service from 1981 to 1986. This method allowed property to be depreciated at a faster rate than had been allowed previously. The modified accelerated cost recovery system (MACRS) replaced ACRS for assets placed into service after 1986.

Accelerated depreciation

A depreciation method that allows you to deduct a greater portion of the cost of depreciable property in the first years after the property is placed in service, rather than spreading the cost evenly over the life of the asset, as with the straight-line depreciation method.

Accommodator

An unrelated party (transunion exchange corporation) who participates in the tax-deferred, like-kind exchange to facilitate the disposition of the exchangor's relinquished property and the acquisition of the exchangor's replacement property. The accommodator has no economic interest except for any compensation (exchange fee) it may receive for acting as an accommodator in facilitating the exchange as defined in section 1031 of the internal revenue code. The accommodator is technically referred to as the qualified intermediary, but is also known as the accommodator, facilitator or intermediary.

Actual receipt
Direct access to your exchange funds or other property. Receiving exchange funds during the exchange period will disqualify your exchange. (See constructive receipt.)

Adjusted cost basis
The amount you use to determine your capital gain or loss from a sale or disposition of property. To determine the adjusted cost basis for your property, you must start with the original purchase cost. You then add your purchasing expenses, your cost of capital improvements and principal payments of special assessments (sewer and streets) to the property, and then subtract depreciation you have taken or were allowed to take, any casualty losses taken and/or any demolition losses taken.

After-tax return
The return from an investment after tax liabilities have been factored in.

Agent
An entity that acts on behalf of the taxpayer. A qualified intermediary cannot be your agent at the time of or during a tax-deferred, like-kind exchange. For 1031 exchange purposes, an agent includes your employee, attorney, accountant or investment banker, or real estate agent or broker within the two-year period prior to the transfer of your first relinquished property. An agency relationship does not exist with entities that offer section 1031 exchanges services or routine title, escrow, trust or financial services. (See related party.)

Alternative minimum tax

A method of calculating income tax that does not allow certain deductions, credits and exclusions. The alternative minimum tax was devised to ensure that individuals, trusts and estates that benefit from tax preferences do not avoid paying any federal income taxes.

Asset

Anything owned that has monetary value.

Asset allocation

Repositioning assets within a portfolio to maximize a return for a specific level of risk.

Asset class

A category of investments that contain similar characteristics.

Balancing the exchange

A balanced exchange ensures that the taxpayer defers 100% of his or her taxes on capital gain and depreciation recapture. To achieve a balanced exchange 1) acquire a replacement property that is equal to or greater than the relinquished property; 2) reinvest all of the net equity from the relinquished property in the replacement property; and 3) assume debt on the replacement property that is equal to or greater than the debt on the replacement property or contribute cash to make up the deficiency. (See partial tax deferment; boot and mortgage boot/relief.)

Basis

The original purchase price or cost of your property plus any out-of-pocket expenses, such as brokerage commissions, escrow costs, title insurance premiums, sales tax (if personal property), and other closing costs directly related to the acquisition.

Beneficiary

An individual, company, organization or other entity named in a trust, life insurance policy, annuity, will or other agreement who receives a financial benefit upon the death of the principal. A beneficiary can be an individual, company, organization, etc.

Bond

Evidence of debt in which the issuer promises to pay the bond-holders a specified amount of interest and to repay the principal at maturity. Bonds are usually issued in multiples of $1,000.

Boot

Non-like-kind property (cash or other property) given by one party to another party in a tax-deferred, like-kind exchange that is taxable. For instance, if you trade in a delivery truck on a new model, the cash you pay in addition to your old truck is boot. Boot received may be offset by boot given. (See also mortgage boot.)

Build-to-suit exchange

A tax-deferred, like-kind exchange whereby the qualified intermediary and/or exchange accommodation titleholder acquires title and holds title to the replacement property on behalf of the exchangor, during which time structures or improvements are constructed or installed on or within the replacement property. Also known as an improvement exchange.

Business assets

Real property, tangible depreciable property, intangible property and other types of property contained or used in a business. Exchanging one business for another business is not permitted under internal revenue code section 1031. However, taxpayers may exchange business assets on an asset-by-asset basis, usually as part of a mixed-property (multi-asset) exchange.

Capital gain or loss
The difference between the selling price of a property or asset and its adjusted cost basis.

Capital gain tax
Tax levied by federal and state governments on investments that are held for one year or more. Investments may include real estate, stocks, bonds, collectibles and tangible depreciable personal property. (See income tax.)

Capital improvements
For land or buildings, improvements (also known as capital improvements) are the expenses of permanently upgrading your property rather than maintaining or repairing it. Instead of taking a deduction for the cost of improvements in the year paid, you add the cost of the improvements to the basis of the property. If the property you improved is a building that is being depreciated, you must depreciate the improvements over the same useful life as the building.

Capitalization rate
The rate of return an investor wants to achieve on real property. The capitalization rate can provide for the return of the investment and the return on the investment (profit). To obtain a property's capitalization rate, divide the net operating income of a property by its value. To determine a property's value, divide the property's net operating income by the desired capitalization rate. In the income-capitalization method of real property appraisal, a capitalization rate is used to appraise a property's value. The income-capitalization method of appraisal is used to value investment property, such as apartment buildings, commercial office buildings and retail malls. (See net operating income.)

Cash equivalents
Short-term investments, such as US treasury securities, certificates of deposit, and money market fund shares, that can easily be liquidated into cash.

Charitable lead trust
A trust established for the benefit of a charitable organization under which the charitable organization receives income from an asset for a set number of years or for the trustor's lifetime. Upon the termination of the trust, the asset reverts to the trustor or to his or her designated heirs. This type of trust can reduce estate taxes and allows the trustor's heirs to retain control of the assets.

Charitable remainder trust
A trust established for the benefit of a charitable organization under which the trustor receives income from an asset for a set number of years or for the trustor's lifetime. Upon the termination of the trust, the asset reverts to the charitable organization. The trustor receives a charitable contribution deduction in the year in which the trust is established, and the assets placed in the trust are exempt from capital gain tax.

Collectibles
Personal property, such as baseball cards, coins, stamps, works of art and memorabilia that is held for investment. Collectibles are exchangeable under internal revenue code section 1031.

Community property
All property acquired by a husband and wife during their marriage. Each spouse has a right to an equal interest in the property. Gifts and inheritances received by an individual spouse during the marriage are treated as separate property. Property acquired by the spouse prior to marriage, property acquired with separate property or rents or profits generated from

separate property are treated as separate property. Arizona, California, Idaho, Louisiana, Nevada, New Mexico, Texas, Washington, and Wisconsin are community property states.

Concurrent exchange

A tax-deferred, like-kind exchange transaction whereby the disposition of the relinquished property and the acquisition of the replacement property close or transfer at the same time. A concurrent exchange is also referred to as a simultaneous exchange.

Condominium

A form of real estate ownership, usually residential property, in which the owners own their proportionate share of a fee interest, as well as an undivided proportionate share of all common areas.

Constructive receipt

Exercising control over your exchange funds or other property. Control over your exchange funds includes having money or property from the exchange credited to your bank account or property or funds reserved for you. Being in constructive receipt of exchange funds or property may result in the disallowance of the tax-deferred, like-kind exchange transaction, thereby creating a taxable sale. (See actual receipt.)

Cooperation clause

Language to be included in the purchase and sale contracts for both relinquished and replacement property that indicates and discloses that the transaction is part of an intended tax-deferred, like-kind exchange transaction and requires that all parties cooperate in completing said exchange.

Cooperatives

A form of real estate ownership, usually residential property, in which individual owners hold shares of stock in a corporation.

Each owner leases property from the corporation under a proprietary lease.

Corporation
A separate entity created by law. Investors in the corporation hold shares of stock. The corporation benefits from any profits generated and is responsible for any losses received. Shareholders may receive dividends on stock and incur any appreciation or depreciation on the sale of their shares of stock. Shareholders are not liable for any debts incurred by the corporation. Creditors can attach a shareholder's shares in the corporation.

Deduction
An amount that can be subtracted from gross income, from a gross estate, or from a gift, lowering the amount on which tax is assessed.

Deferred exchange
The sale or disposition of real estate or personal property (relinquished property) and the acquisition of like-kind real estate or personal property (replacement property) structured as a tax-deferred, like-kind exchange transaction pursuant to section 1031 of the internal revenue code and section 1.1031 of the treasury regulations in order to defer federal, and in most cases state, capital gain and depreciation recapture taxes.

Delaware statutory trust (DST)
A Delaware statutory trust is a separate legal entity created as a trust under Delaware law in which each owner has a beneficial interest for federal income tax purposes and is treated as owning an undivided fractional interest in the property. In 2004, the IRS released revenue ruling 2004 – 86, which allows the use of a DST to acquire real estate where the beneficial interest in the trust will be treated as direct interest in replacement property for purposes of conducting 1031 exchanges.

Delayed exchange

A tax-deferred, like-kind exchange where there is a delay or period of time between the close and transfer of the exchangor's relinquished property and replacement property.

Depreciable property

Property with a useful life of more than one year that is held for investment or used in your trade or business. You spread the cost of the asset over its estimated useful life rather than deducting the entire cost in the year that you placed the asset in service. (See depreciation recapture for more information regarding the sale or disposition of assets that have been depreciated.)

Depreciation

Periodic wearing away of property over the property's economic life. The IRS requires investors and business owners to take a tax deduction on the amount of a property's depreciation. The practice of amortizing or spreading the cost of depreciable property over a specified period of time, usually its estimated depreciable life. To put it another way, you are allowed a deduction on your income tax return for the wearing away and expensing over time of property or assets, such as aircraft, vehicles, livestock and buildings. A depreciable asset is a capital expenditure in depreciable property used in a trade or business or held for the production of income and has a definite useful life of more than one year. Non-depreciable property includes vacant land. For assets that have an expected useful life of more than one year, you spread the cost of the asset over its estimated useful life rather than deducting the entire cost in the year you place the asset in service. The tax code (law) specifies the depreciation period for specific types of assets.

Depreciation recapture

The amount of gain resulting from the disposition of property that represents the recovery of depreciation expense that has been previously deducted on the taxpayer's (exchangor's) income tax returns.

Direct deeding

A practice authorized by treasury revenue ruling 90-34 whereby either the relinquished property or the replacement property can be deeded directly from seller to buyer without deeding the property to the qualified intermediary. (See sequential deeding for industry practices prior to treasury revenue ruling 90-34.)

Disposition

The sale or other disposal of property that causes a gain or a loss including like-kind exchanges and involuntary conversions.

Dividend

A pro-rata portion of earnings distributed in cash by a contribution to its stockholders. In preferred stock, dividends are usually fixed; with common shares, dividends may vary with the performance of the company.

Eat

Acronym for exchange accommodation titleholder. (See exchange accommodation titleholder.)

Equity

The value of a person's ownership in real property or securities; the market value of a property or business, less any claims or liens on it.

Exchange

The sale or disposition of real estate or personal property (relinquished property) and the acquisition of like-kind real estate or personal property (replacement property) structured as a tax-deferred, like-kind exchange transaction pursuant to section 1031 of the internal revenue code and section 1.1031 of the treasury regulations in order to defer federal, and in most cases state, capital gain and depreciation recapture taxes.

Exchange accommodation titleholder ("eat")

An unrelated party (transunion reverse exchange corporation) that holds the qualified indicia of ownership (customarily the title) of either the replacement or relinquished property in order to facilitate a reverse and/or build-to-suit tax-deferred, like-kind exchange transaction pursuant to revenue procedure 2000-37.

Exchange agreement

A written agreement between the qualified intermediary and exchangor setting forth the exchangor's intent to exchange relinquished property for replacement property, as well as the terms, conditions and responsibilities of each party pursuant to the tax-deferred, like-kind exchange transaction.

Exchange period

The period of time during which the exchangor must complete the acquisition of the replacement property(ies) in his or her tax-deferred, like-kind exchange transaction. The exchange period is 180 calendar days from the transfer of the exchangor's first relinquished property, or the due date (including extensions) of the exchangor's income tax return for the year in which the tax-deferred, like-kind exchange transaction took place, whichever is earlier, and is not extended due to holidays or weekends.

Exchangor

The taxpayer who is completing the tax-deferred, like-kind exchange transaction. An exchangor may be an individual, partnership, LLC, corporation, institution or business.

Excluded property

The rules for like-kind exchanges do not apply to property held for personal use (such as homes, boats or cars); cash; stock in trade or other property held primarily for sale (such as inventories, raw materials and real estate held by dealers); stocks, bonds, notes or other securities or evidences of indebtedness (such as accounts receivable); partnership interests; certificates of trust or beneficial interest; chooses in action.

Fair market value
The price at which property would change hands between a buyer and a seller, neither having to buy or sell, and both having reasonable knowledge of all necessary facts.

Fixed income
Income from investments, such as CDs, social security benefits, pension benefits, some annuities, or most bonds, that is the same every month.

Fractional interest
An undivided fractional interest or partial interest in property. (See also tenancy-in-common interest.)

Going concern value
Additional value that attaches to property because the property is an integral part of an ongoing business activity. It includes value based on the ability of a business to continue to function and generate business even though there is a change in ownership.

Goodwill
The value of a business or trade based on continued customer patronage due to its name, reputation or any other factor. The goodwill of a business is not exchangeable under internal revenue code section 1031.

Gross multiplier
A variation on the income-capitalization method of appraising property. The gross multiplier approach is a way to obtain a fast, rough estimate of a property's value. In this approach, a monthly or annual number is multiplied by a property's gross

income to obtain the property's value. Dividing the sale price of a similar property by its gross income provides its gross multiplier.

Identification period

The period of time during which the exchangor must identify potential replacement properties in his or her tax-deferred, like-kind exchange. The period is 45 calendar days from the transfer of the exchangor's relinquished property and is not extended due to holidays or weekends.

Improvement exchange

A tax-deferred, like-kind exchange whereby the qualified intermediary and/or exchange accommodation titleholder acquires title and holds title to the replacement property on behalf of exchangor, during which time new or additional structures or improvements are constructed or installed on or within the replacement property. Also known as a build-to-suit exchange.

Improvements

For land or buildings, improvements (also known as capital improvements) are the expenses of permanently upgrading your property rather than maintaining or repairing it. Instead of taking a deduction for the cost of improvements in the year paid, you add the cost of the improvements to the basis of the property. If the property you improved is a building that is being depreciated, you must depreciate the improvements over the same useful life as the building.

Income tax

Taxes owed to the federal government based upon the taxpayer's income, including income derived from a property sale. In a 1031 exchange, income generated when property is transferred is not immediately taxed. The income tax is deferred until a new taxable event occurs.

Intangible personal property

Property that does not have value itself but represents something else. Trademarks, patents and franchises are examples of intangible property. Aircraft, business furniture and equipment are examples of tangible personal property.

Intermediary

An unrelated party (transunion exchange corporation) who participates in the tax-deferred, like-kind exchange to facilitate the disposition of the exchangor's relinquished property and the acquisition of the exchangor's replacement property. The intermediary has no economic interest except for any compensation (exchange fee) it may receive for acting as an intermediary in facilitating the exchange as defined in section 1031 of the internal revenue code. The intermediary is technically referred to as the qualified intermediary, but is also known as the accommodator, facilitator or intermediary.

Internal revenue code 1031

Section 1031 of the internal revenue code allows an exchangor to defer his or her capital gain tax and depreciation recapture tax when he or she exchanges relinquished property for like-kind or like-class replacement property.

Irrevocable trust

A trust that may not be modified or terminated by the trustor after its creation.

IRS

Internal Revenue Service

Joint tenancy

Two or more individuals who own an undivided equal interest in a piece of property. Four unities are required to create a joint tenancy:

Time–all joint tenants must obtain their interest at one time

Title–all must obtain their interest by the same document

Interest–each joint tenant has an equal share in ownership

Possession–each joint tenant has an equal right of possession. If one of the joint tenants dies, his or her interest passes automatically to the surviving party or parties. No inheritance taxes or probate proceedings are required. No joint tenant can sell his or her ownership interest without terminating the joint tenancy.

Like-class and like-kind personal property

Refers to the nature or character of the property and not to its grade or quality.

Like-kind exchange
The sale or disposition of real estate (relinquished property) and the acquisition of like-kind real estate or personal property (replacement property) structured as a tax-deferred, like-kind exchange transaction pursuant to section 1031 of the internal revenue code and section 1.1031 of the treasury regulations in order to defer federal, and in most cases state, capital gain and depreciation recapture taxes.

Like-kind property
Property that is exchangeable with another property. Refers to the nature or character of the property and not to its grade or quality.

Limited liability company (LLC)
Members of limited liability companies enjoy the limited liability offered by corporations and the minimum requirements of an s corporation. Limited liability companies typically contain two or more members and must file articles of organization

with the secretary of state, although single-member LLCs are allowed in certain states.

Limited partnership (LP)

Investors who pool their money to develop or purchase income-producing properties. Income from these properties is distributed as dividend payments. In a limited partnership, each limited partner's liability is limited to the amount of his or her investment. A limited partner only contributes money and is not actively involved in the business. A limited partnership must have one general partner, who is personally liable for all debts.

Living trusts

A trust created by an individual or individuals, often a husband and wife, during his or her lifetime. Often these individuals hold property as joint trustees for their benefit. If one spouse dies, the surviving spouse would hold title to the property as a trustee. When the surviving spouse dies, the property would pass to the beneficiaries of the trust. Holding property in a living trust allows the heirs to avoid probate and inheritance taxes.

Mixed property (multi-asset) exchange

An exchange that contains different types of properties, such as depreciable tangible personal property, real property, and intangible personal property. In a mixed property exchange, relinquished properties are segmented in like-kind groups and matched with corresponding like-kind groups of replacement properties.

Modified accelerated cost recovery system (MACRS)

The depreciation method generally used since 1986 for writing off the value of depreciable property, other than real estate, over time. MACRS allows you to write off the cost of assets faster than the straight-line depreciation method.

Mortgage boot/relief

When you assume debt on your replacement property that is less than the debt on your relinquished property, you receive mortgage boot or mortgage relief. Generally speaking, mortgage boot received triggers the recognition of gain and is taxable, unless offset by cash boot added or given up in the exchange. (See boot.)

Multiple property exchange

Disposition and/or acquisition of more than one property in a section 1031 exchange.

Napkin test

A simple exercise to determine the potential for exposing taxable assets or "boot" in an exchange. The napkin test compares the value, equity and mortgage of the relinquished and replacement properties. By going across or up in value, equity and mortgage there is no taxable boot in the exchange.

The calculations are based off the following: if when subtracting the relinquished property value from the replacement property value a zero or positive amount is given, then there is no taxable boot. If a negative amount is given, then taxes are paid on that amount.

Net operating income

A property's gross income (scheduled rents and 100% vacancy factor) less its total annual expenses (including management costs, utilities, services, repairs, a vacancy factor, and a credit loss factor) plus any additional other income (vending machines, coin laundry operations, etc.). Principal and interest payments on the mortgage and tax liability are not included.

Ordinary income tax

Tax levied by federal and state governments on a taxpayer's adjusted gross income. Investments that are held for less than one year are taxed at ordinary income tax rates. (See capital gain tax.)

Parking arrangement

A process or procedure whereby either the exchangor's relinquished property or replacement property is acquired by an exchange accommodation titleholder ("eat") in order to facilitate a reverse and/or build-to-suit tax-deferred, like-kind exchange transaction pursuant to treasury revenue ruling 2000-37.

Partial exchange

An exchange that entails receiving cash, excluded property and/or non-like-kind property and/or any net reduction in debt (mortgage relief) on the replacement property, as well as an exchange of qualified, like-kind property. In the case of a partial exchange, tax liability would be incurred on the non-qualifying portion and capital gain deferred on the qualifying portion under internal revenue code section 1031.

Partial tax deferment

A tax that is owed by the taxpayer, of which part of the tax is paid to the IRS when taxes are due. The remaining tax is postponed to a time when a new taxable event occurs.

Partnership (tenancy in partnership)

An association of two or more persons who engage in a business for profit. A partnership is created by an agreement, which does not have to be in writing. However, for the partnership to hold title in a partnership name, the partnership agreement must be signed, acknowledged and recorded. Tenancy in partnership allows any number of partners to have equal or unequal interest in property in relation to their interests in the partnership. Profits and liabilities are passed through to the members. In a limited partnership, each limited partner's liability is limited to the amount of his or her investment. A limited partner only contributes money and is not actively involved in the business. A limited partnership must have one general partner who is personally liable for all debts. Partnership entities can complete exchanges. Partnership interests are not exchangeable. Difficulties sometimes occur in 1031 exchanges when some partners want to enter into an exchange while others want to sell.

Personal property exchange (check with your tax advisor as 2018 this is no longer available)
A tax-deferred transfer of personal property (relinquished property) for other personal property (replacement property) that are of like-kind or like-class to each other.

Principal residence exemption
Exclusion from capital gain tax on the sale of principal residence of $250,000 for individual taxpayers and $500,000 for couples, filing jointly, under internal revenue code section 121. Property must have been the principal residence of the taxpayer(s) 24 months out of the last 60 months. In the case of a dual-use property, such as a ranch, retail store, duplex or triplex, the taxpayer can defer taxes on the portion of the property used for business or investment under internal revenue code section 1031 and exclude capital gain on the portion used as the primary residence under section 121.

Qualified escrow account
An escrow account, wherein the escrow agent (diversified title insurance company) is not the exchangor or a disqualified person and that limits the exchangor's rights to receive, pledge, borrow or otherwise obtain the benefits of the tax-deferred, like-kind exchange cash balance and/or other assets from the sale of the relinquished property in compliance with the treasury regulations. The qualified escrow account also ensures that the exchangor's exchange funds and/or assets are held as fiduciary funds and are therefore protected against claims from potential creditors of the qualified intermediary.

Qualified exchange accommodation arrangement

The contractual arrangement between the exchangor and the exchange accommodator titleholder whereby each holds a parked property pursuant to revenue procedure 2000-37.

Qualified exchange accommodation agreement

The actual contract or agreement between the exchangor and the exchange accommodator titleholder that outlines the terms for parking property pursuant to revenue procedure 2000-37.

Qualified intermediary

An unrelated party (transunion exchange corporation) who participates in the tax-deferred, like-kind exchange to facilitate the disposition of the exchangor's relinquished property and the acquisition of the exchangor's replacement property. The qualified intermediary has no economic interest except for any compensation (exchange fee) it may receive for facilitating the exchange as defined in section 1031 of the internal revenue code. The qualified intermediary is the correct technical reference pursuant to treasury regulations, but the qualified intermediary is also known as the accommodator, facilitator or intermediary.

Qualified trust account

A trust, wherein the trustee is not the exchangor or a disqualified person and that limits the exchangor's rights to receive, pledge, borrow or otherwise obtain the benefits of the tax-deferred, like-kind exchange cash balance and/or other assets from the sale of the relinquished property in compliance with the treasury regulations. The qualified trust account also ensures that the exchangor's exchange funds and/or assets are held as fiduciary funds and are therefore protected against claims from potential creditors of the qualified intermediary.

Qualified use

An exchangor must intend to use the property in their trade or business, to hold the property for investment or to hold the property for income production in order to satisfy the qualified use test.

Real property

Land and buildings (improvements), including but not limited to homes, apartment buildings, shopping centers, commercial buildings, factories, condominiums, leases of 30-years or more, quarries, and oil fields. All types of real property are exchangeable for all other types of real property. In general, state law determines what constitutes real property.

Real estate investment trust (REIT)

A trust that invests primarily in real estate and mortgages and passes income, losses and other tax items to its investors. REITs are typically classified as a security and are therefore not exchangeable.

Real property exchange

The sale or disposition of real estate (relinquished property) and the acquisition of like-kind real estate (replacement property) structured as a tax-deferred, like-kind exchange transaction pursuant to section 1031 of the internal revenue code and section 1.1031 of treasury regulations in order to defer federal, and in most cases state, capital gain and depreciation recapture taxes.

Related party

Individuals and/or business entities determined by section 267(b) of the internal revenue code as having a special connection to the taxpayer/exchanger. A transaction between a related party and an exchanger may be restricted or prohibited in a 1031 exchange. Related parties include family members (spouses, children, siblings, parents or grandparents, but not aunts, uncles, cousins or ex-spouses) and a corporation in which you have more than a 50% ownership; or a partnership or two partnerships in which you directly or indirectly own more than a 50% share of the capital or profits.

Relinquished property
The property to be sold or disposed of by the exchangor in the tax-deferred, like-kind exchange transaction.

Replacement property
The like-kind property to be acquired or received by the exchangor in the tax-deferred, like-kind exchange transaction.

Reverse exchange
A tax-deferred, like-kind exchange transaction whereby the replacement property is acquired first and the disposition of the relinquished property occurs at a later date.

Reverse/improvement exchange
The eat can make improvements to the replacement property before transferring it to the taxpayer as part of a reverse exchange.

Revocable trust
A trust in which the creator reserves the right to modify or terminate the trust at any time.

S corporation
A small, closely held corporation (75 or fewer investors) who elect to be taxed as a partnership where shareholders pay taxes on all earnings. This avoids double taxation of corporate income and dividend income that occurs in corporations.

Safe harbors
Treasury regulations provide certain safe harbors that assist qualified intermediaries and exchangors in structuring tax-deferred, like-kind exchange transactions so they can be assured

that no constructive receipt issues will be encountered during the exchange cycle.

Seller carry-back financing

When the buyer of a property gives the seller of the property a note, secured by a deed of trust or mortgage. In a section 1031 exchange, seller carry-back financing is treated as boot, unless it is sold at a discount on the secondary market or assigned to the seller as a down payment on the replacement property.

Sequential deeding

The former practice of transferring or deeding title to the exchangor's relinquished property to the qualified intermediary first and then sequentially and immediately transferring or deeding title from the qualified intermediary to the buyer in order to properly structure a tax-deferred, like-kind exchange prior to the issuance of treasury revenue ruling 90-34. Sequential deeding is used only in special tax-deferred, like-kind exchange transactions today that require special structuring. (See direct deeding for the current day practice.)

Simultaneous exchange

A tax-deferred, like-kind exchange transaction whereby the disposition of the relinquished property and the acquisition of the replacement property close or transfer at the same time. A simultaneous exchange is also referred to as a concurrent exchange.

Starker exchange

Another common name for the tax-deferred, like-kind exchange transaction based on a court decision that was handed down (Starker vs. Commissioner) in 1979. The Ninth Circuit Court of Appeals eventually agreed with Starker that its delayed tax-deferred, like-kind exchange transaction did in fact constitute a valid exchange pursuant to section 1031 of the internal revenue code. This ruling set the precedent for our current day delayed exchange structures.

Straight-line depreciation method
A depreciation method that spreads the cost or other basis of property evenly over its estimated useful life.

Tangible personal property
Property other than real estate that physically exists. Aircraft, business equipment and vehicles are examples of tangible personal property. Assets such as trademarks, patents and franchises only represent value and are therefore intangible property.

Tax-deferral
The postponement of taxes to a later year, usually by recognizing income or a gain at a later time. Tax-deferred, like-kind exchange transactions are a common method of deferring capital gain and depreciation recapture taxes.

Tax-deferred exchange
The sale or disposition of real estate or personal property (relinquished property) and the acquisition of like-kind real estate or personal property (replacement property) structured as a tax-deferred, like-kind exchange transaction pursuant to section 1031 of the internal revenue code and section 1.1031 of treasury regulations in order to defer federal, and in most cases state, capital gain and depreciation recapture taxes.

Taxpayer
The person or entity that is completing the tax-deferred, like-kind exchange transaction, commonly referred to as the exchangor.

Tenancy-in-common interest (co-tenancy) (TIC)
A separate, undivided fractional interest in property. A tenancy-in-common interest is made up of two or more individuals,

who have equal rights of possession. Co-tenants' interests may be equal or unequal and may be created at different times and through the use of different conveyances. Each co-tenant has the right to dispose of or encumber his or her interest without the agreement of the other co-tenants. He or she cannot, however, encumber the entire property without the consent of all of the co-tenants. In an internal revenue code section 1031 exchange, an exchangor may acquire a tenancy-in-common interest with one or more other investors, as his or her like-kind replacement property. For purposes of internal revenue code section 1031 exchanges, a co-tenancy must only engage in investment activities, including supporting services that would typically accompany the investment. Co-tenants that are engaging in separate business activities are treated as partnerships by the IRS

Tenancy in severalty
Separate ownership of property by one person.

Titleholder
The entity that owns/holds title to property. In an internal revenue code section 1031 exchange, the titleholder of the relinquished property must generally be the same as the titleholder of the replacement property. If a taxpayer dies prior to the acquisition of the replacement property, his or her estate may complete the exchange. When the acquisition and disposition entities bear the same taxpayer identification numbers, such as disregarded entities (single-member LLCs and revocable living trusts), the exchange usually qualifies.

Trust
A legal entity created by an individual in which one person or institution holds the right to manage property or assets for the benefit of someone else.

Trustee

An individual or institution appointed to administer a trust for its beneficiaries.

Glossary terms courtesy of Equity Advantage, www.1031exchange.com.

Appendix I

Section 1031 – Exchange of property held for productive use or investment

Nonrecognition of gain or loss from exchanges solely in kind

(1) In general

No gain or loss shall be recognized on the exchange of property held for productive use in a trade or business or for investment if such property is exchanged solely for property of like kind which is to be held either for productive use in a trade or business or for investment.

(2) Exception

This subsection shall not apply to any exchange of— (a) stock in trade or other property held primarily for sale, (b) stocks, bonds or notes, (c) other securities or evidences of indebtedness or interest, (d) interests in a partnership, (e) certificates of trust or beneficial interests, or (f) chooses in action. For purposes of this section, an interest in a partnership which has in effect a valid election under section 761 (a) to be excluded from the application of all of subchapter k shall be treated as an interest in each of the assets of such partnership and not as an interest in a partnership.

(3) Requirement that property be identified and that exchange be completed not more than 180 days after transfer of exchanged property.

For purposes of this subsection, any property received by the taxpayer shall be treated as property which is not like-kind property if— (a) such property is not identified as property to be received in the exchange on or before the day which is 45 days after the date on which the taxpayer transfers the property relinquished in the exchange, or (b) such property is received after the earlier of — (i) the day which is 180 days after the date on which the taxpayer transfers the property relinquished in the exchange, or (ii) the due date (determined with regard to extension) for the transferor's return of the tax imposed by this chapter for the taxable year in which the transfer of the relinquished property occurs.

Gain from exchanges not solely in kind

If an exchange would be within the provisions of subsection (a), of section 1035(a), of section 1036(a), or of section 1037(a), if it were not for the fact that the property received in exchange consists not only of property permitted by such provisions to be received without the recognition of gain, but also of other property or money, then the gain, if any, to the recipient shall be recognized, but in an amount not in excess of the sum of such money and the fair market value of such other property.

Loss from exchanges not solely in kind
If an exchange would be within the provisions of subsection (a), of section 1035(a), of section 1036(a), or of section 1037(a), if it were not for the fact that the property received in exchange consists not only of property permitted by such provisions to be received without the recognition of gain or loss, but also of other property or money, then no loss from the exchange shall be recognized.

Basis
If property was acquired on an exchange described in this section, section 1035(a), section 1036(a), or section 1037(a), then

the basis shall be the same as that of the property exchanged, decreased in the amount of any money received by the taxpayer and increased in the amount of gain or decreased in the amount of loss to the taxpayer that was recognized on such exchange. If the property so acquired consisted in part of the type of property permitted by this section, section 1035(a), section 1036(a), or section 1037(a), to be received without the recognition of gain or loss, and in part of other property, the basis provided in this subsection shall be allocated between the properties (other than money) received, and for the purpose of the allocation there shall be assigned to such other property an amount equivalent to its fair market value at the date of the exchange. For purposes of this section, section 1035(a), and section 1036(a), where as part of the consideration to the taxpayer another party to the exchange assumed (as determined under section 357(d)) a liability of the taxpayer, such assumption shall be considered as money received by the taxpayer on the exchange. Exchanges of livestock of different sexes for purposes of this section, livestock of different sexes are not property of a like kind.

Special rules for exchanges between related persons

(1) In general

If — (a) a taxpayer exchanges property with a related person, (b) there is nonrecognition of gain or loss to the taxpayer under this section with respect to the exchange of such property (determined without regard to this subsection), and (c) before the date 2 years after the date of the last transfer which was part of such exchange— (i) the related person disposes of such property, or (ii) the taxpayer disposes of the property received in the exchange from the related person which was of like kind to the property transferred by the taxpayer, there shall be no nonrecognition of gain or loss under this section to the taxpayer with respect to such exchange; except that any gain or loss recognized by the taxpayer by reason of this subsection shall be taken into account as of the date on which the disposition referred to in subparagraph (c) occurs.

(2) Certain dispositions not taken into account

For purposes of paragraph (1)(c), there shall not be taken into account any disposition — (a) after the earlier of the death of the taxpayer or the death of the related person, (b) in a compulsory or involuntary conversion (within the meaning of section 1033) if the exchange occurred before the threat or imminence of such conversion, or (c) with respect to which it is established to the satisfaction of the secretary that neither the exchange nor such disposition had as one of its principal purposes the avoidance of federal income tax.

(3) Related person

For purposes of this subsection, the term "related person" means any person bearing a relationship to the taxpayer described in section 267 (b) or 707 (b)(1).

(4) Treatment of certain transactions

This section shall not apply to any exchange, which is part of a transaction (or series of transactions) structured to avoid the purposes of this subsection.

Special rule where substantial diminution of risk

(1) In general

If paragraph (2) applies to any property for any period, the running of the period set forth in subsection (f)(1)

(c) with respect to such property shall be suspended during such period.

(2) Property to which subsection applies

This paragraph shall apply to any property for any period during which the holder's risk of loss with respect to the property is substantially diminished by—(a) the holding of a put with respect to such property, (b) the holding by another person of a right to acquire such property, or (c) a short sale or any other transaction.

Special rules for foreign real and personal property

For purposes of this section—

(1) Real property

Real property located in the United States and real property located outside the United States are not property of a like kind.

(2) Personal property

(a) In general

Personal property used predominantly within the United States and personal property used predominantly outside the United States are not property of a like kind.

(b) Predominant use

Except as provided in subparagraphs (c) and (d), the predominant use of any property shall be determined based on—(i) in the case of the property relinquished in the exchange, the 2-year period ending on the date of such relinquishment, and (ii) in the case of the property acquired in the exchange, the 2-year period beginning on the date of such acquisition.

(c) Property held for less than 2 years

Except in the case of an exchange which is part of a transaction (or series of transactions) structured to avoid the purposes of this subsection— (i) only the periods the property was held by the person relinquishing the property (or any related person) shall be taken into account under subparagraph (b)(i), and (ii) only the periods the property was held by the person acquiring the property (or any related person) shall be taken into account under subparagraph (b)(ii).

(d) Special rule for certain property

Property described in any subparagraph of section 168 (g)(4) shall be treated as used predominantly in the United States.

Appendix II

Internal Revenue Service (I.R.S.)

Revenue Ruling (Rev. Rul.)

Released: July 20, 2004 Published: August 16, 2004

Classification of Delaware Statutory Trust

Section 671 - trust income, deductions and credits attributable to grantors and others as substantial owners
How will certain Delaware Statutory Trusts be classified for federal tax purposes and may a taxpayer acquire an interest in certain Delaware Statutory Trusts without recognition of gain or loss under section 1031 of the internal revenue code.

Section 677 - income for benefit of grantor
How will certain Delaware Statutory Trusts be classified for federal tax purposes and may a taxpayer acquire an interest in certain Delaware Statutory Trusts without recognition of gain or loss under section 1031 of the internal revenue code.

Section 761 - terms defined
How will certain Delaware Statutory Trusts be classified for federal tax purposes and may a taxpayer acquire an interest in certain Delaware Statutory Trusts without recognition of gain or loss under section 1031 of the internal revenue code.

Section 1031 - exchange of property held for productive use or investment
How will certain Delaware Statutory Trusts be classified for federal tax purposes and may a taxpayer acquire an interest in certain Delaware Statutory Trusts without recognition of gain or loss under section 1031 of the internal revenue code.

26 CFR 301.7701-1: classification of organizations for federal tax purposes

Classification of Delaware Statutory Trust

This ruling explains how a Delaware Statutory Trust described in the ruling will be classified for federal tax purposes and whether a taxpayer may acquire an interest in the Delaware Statutory Trust without recognition of gain or loss under section 1031 of the code. Rev. Ruls. 78-371 and 92-105 distinguished.

Issue(s)
(1) In the situation described below, how is a Delaware Statutory Trust, described in Del. Code ann. Title 12, sections 3801 - 3824, classified for federal tax purposes.

(2) In the situation described below, may a taxpayer exchange real property for an interest in a Delaware Statutory Trust without recognition of gain or loss under section 1031 of the internal revenue code.

Facts
On January 1, 2005, a, an individual, borrows money from BK, a bank, and signs a 10-year note bearing adequate stated interest, within the meaning of section 483. On January 1, 2005, a uses the proceeds of the loan to purchase Blackacre, rental real property. The note is secured by Blackacre and is nonrecourse to a.

Immediately following a's purchase of Blackacre, a enters into a net lease with Z for a term of 10 years. Under the terms of the lease, Z is to pay all taxes, assessments, fees, or other charges imposed on Blackacre by federal, state or local authorities. In addition, Z is to pay all insurance, maintenance, ordinary repairs, and utilities relating to Blackacre. Z may sublease Blackacre. Z's rent is a fixed amount that may be adjusted by a formula described in the lease agreement that is based upon a fixed rate or an objective index, such as an escalator clause based upon the consumer price index, but adjustments to the rate or index are not within the control of any of the parties to the lease. Z's rent is not contingent on Z's ability to lease the property or on Z's gross sales or net profits derived from the property.

Also on January 1, 2005, a forms DST, a Delaware Statutory Trust described in the Delaware Statutory Trust act, del. Code ann. Title 12, sections 3801 - 3824, to hold property for investment. A contributes Blackacre to DST. Upon contribution, DST assumes a's rights and obligations under the note with BK and the lease with Z. In accordance with the terms of the note, neither DST nor any of its beneficial owners are personally liable to BK on the note, which continues to be secured by Blackacre.

The trust agreement provides that interests in DST are freely transferable. However, DST interests are not publicly traded on an established securities market. DST will terminate on the earlier of 10 years from the date of its creation or the disposition of Blackacre, but will not terminate on the bankruptcy, death or incapacity of any owner or on the transfer of any right, title, or interest of the owners. The trust agreement further provides that interests in DST will be of a single class, representing undivided beneficial interests in the assets of DST.

Under the trust agreement, the trustee is authorized to establish a reasonable reserve for expenses associated with holding Blackacre that may be payable out of trust funds. The trustee is required to distribute all available cash less reserves quarterly to each beneficial owner in proportion to their respective interests in DST. The trustee is required to invest cash received from Blackacre between each quarterly distribution and all cash held in reserve in short-term obligations of (or guaranteed by) the

United States, or any agency or instrumentality thereof, and in certificates of deposit of any bank or trust company having a minimum stated surplus and capital. The trustee is permitted to invest only in obligations maturing prior to the next distribution date and is required to hold such obligations until maturity. In addition to the right to a quarterly distribution of cash, each beneficial owner has the right to an in-kind distribution of its proportionate share of trust property.

The trust agreement provides that the trustee's activities are limited to the collection and distribution of income. The trustee may not exchange Blackacre for other property, purchase assets other than the short-term investments described above, or accept additional contributions of assets (including money) to DST. The trustee may not renegotiate the terms of the debt used to acquire Blackacre and may not renegotiate the lease with Z or enter into leases with tenants other than Z, except in the case of Z's bankruptcy or insolvency. In addition, the trustee may make only minor non-structural modifications to Blackacre, unless otherwise required by law. The trust agreement further provides that the trustee may engage in ministerial activities to the extent required to maintain and operate DST under local law.

On January 3, 2005, b and c exchange Whiteacre and Greenacre, respectively, for all of A's interests in DST through a qualified intermediary, within the meaning of section 1.1031(k)-1(g). A does not engage in a section 1031 exchange. Whiteacre and Greenacre were held for investment and are of like kind to Blackacre, within the meaning of section 1031.

Neither DST nor its trustee enters into a written agreement with A, B or C, creating an agency relationship. In dealings with third parties, neither DST nor its trustee is represented as an agent of A, B or C. BK is not related to A, B, C, DST's trustee or Z within the meaning of section 267(b) or section 707(b). Z is not related to B, C or DST's trustee within the meaning of section 267(b) or section 707(b).

Law

Delaware law provides that a Delaware Statutory Trust is an unincorporated association recognized as an entity separate from its owners. A Delaware Statutory Trust is created by executing a governing instrument and filing an executed certificate of trust. Creditors of the beneficial owners of a Delaware Statutory Trust may not assert claims directly against the property in the trust. A Delaware Statutory Trust may sue or be sued, and property held in a Delaware Statutory Trust is subject to attachment or execution as if the trust were a corporation. Beneficial owners of a Delaware Statutory Trust are entitled to the same limitation on personal liability because of actions of the Delaware Statutory Trust that is extended to stockholders of Delaware corporations. A Delaware Statutory Trust may merge or consolidate with or into one or more statutory entities or other business entities.

Section 671 provides that, where the grantor or another person is treated as the owner of any portion of a trust (commonly referred to as a "grantor trust"), there shall be included in computing the taxable income and credits of the grantor or the other person those items of income, deductions and credits against tax of the trust which are attributable to that portion of the trust to the extent that the items would be taken into account under chapter 1 in computing taxable income or credits against the tax of an individual.

Section 1.671-2(e)(1) of the income tax regulations provides that, for purposes of subchapter j, a grantor includes any person to the extent such person either creates a trust or directly or indirectly makes a gratuitous transfer of property to a trust.

Under section 1.671-2(e)(3), the term "grantor" includes any person who acquires an interest in a trust from a grantor of the trust if the interest acquired is an interest in certain investment trusts described in section 301.7701-4(c).

Under section 677(a), the grantor is treated as the owner of any portion of a trust whose income without the approval or consent of any adverse party is, or, in the discretion of the grantor or a nonadverse party, or both, may be distributed, or held or accumulated for future distribution, to the grantor or the grantor's spouse.

A person that is treated as the owner of an undivided fractional interest of a trust under subpart e of part i, subchapter j of the code (section 671 and following), is considered to own the trust assets attributable to that undivided fractional interest of the trust for federal income tax purposes. See rev. Rul. 88-103, 1988-2 C.B. 304; rev. Rul. 85-45, 1985-1 C.B. 183; and rev. Rul. 85-13, 1985-1 C.B. 184. See also section 1.1001-2(c), example 5.

Section 761(a) provides that the term "partnership" includes a syndicate, group, pool, joint venture, or other unincorporated organization through or by means of which any business, financial operation, or venture is carried on, and that is not a corporation or a trust or estate. Under regulations the secretary may, at the election of all the members of the unincorporated organization, exclude such organization from the application of all or part of subchapter k, if the income of the members of the organization may be adequately determined without the computation of partnership taxable income and the organization is availed of (1) for investment purposes only and not for the active conduct of a business, (2) for the joint production, extraction, or use of property, but not for the purpose of selling services or property produced or extracted, or (3) by dealers in securities for a short period for the purpose of underwriting, selling, or distributing a particular issue of securities.

Section 1.761-2(a)(2) provides the requirements that must be satisfied for participants in the joint purchase, retention, sale or exchange of investment property to elect to be excluded from the application of the provisions of subchapter k. One of these requirements is that the participants own the property as co-owners.

Section 1031(a)(1) provides that no gain or loss is recognized on the exchange of property held for productive use in a trade or business or for investment if such property is exchanged solely for property of like kind that is to be held either for productive use in a trade or business or for investment.

Section 1031(a)(2) provides that section 1031(a) does not apply to any exchange of stocks, bonds or notes, other securities or evidences of indebtedness or interest, interests in a partnership, or certificates of trust or beneficial interests. It further provides that an interest in a partnership that has in effect a valid election under section 761(a) to be excluded from the application of all of subchapter k shall be treated as an interest in each of the assets of the partnership and not as an interest in a partnership.

Under section 301.7701-1(a)(1) of the procedure and administration regulations, whether an organization is an entity separate from its owners for federal tax purposes is a matter of federal tax law and does not depend on whether the organization is recognized as an entity under local law.

Generally, when participants in a venture form a state law entity and avail themselves of the benefits of that entity for a valid business purpose, such as investment or profit, and not for tax avoidance, the entity will be recognized for federal tax purposes. See Moline Properties, Inc. V. Comm'r, 319 U.S. 436 (1943); Zmuda v. Comm'r, 731 f.2d 1417 (9th Cir. 1984); Boca Investerings

P'ship v. United States, 314 f.3d 625 (D.C. Cir. 2003); Saba P'ship v. Comm'r, 273 f.3d 1135 (D.C. Cir. 2001); Asa Investerings P'ship v. Comm'r, 201 f.3d 505 (D.C. Cir. 2000); Markosian v. Comm'r, 73 T.C. 1235 (1980).

Section 301.7701-2(a) defines the term "business entity" as any entity recognized for federal tax purposes (including an entity with a single owner that may be disregarded as an entity separate from its owner under section 301.7701- 3) that is not properly classified as a trust under section 301.7701-4 or otherwise subject to special treatment under the code. A business entity with two or more owners is classified for federal tax purposes as either a corporation or a partnership. A business entity with only one owner is classified as a corporation or is disregarded.

Section 301.7701-3(a) provides that an eligible entity can elect its classification for federal tax purposes. Under section 301.7701-3(b)(1), unless the entity elects otherwise, a domestic eligible entity is a partnership if it has two or more owners or is disregarded as an entity separate from its owner if it has a single owner.

Section 301.7701-4(a) provides that the term "trust" refers to an arrangement created either by will or by an inter vivos declaration whereby trustees take title to property for the purpose of protecting and conserving it for the beneficiaries. Usually the beneficiaries of a trust do no more than accept the benefits thereof and are not voluntary planners or creators of the trust arrangement. However, the beneficiaries of a trust may be the persons who create it, and it will be recognized as a trust if it was created for the purpose of protecting and conserving the trust property for beneficiaries who stand in the same relation to the trust as they would if the trust had been created by others for them.

Section 301.7701-4(b) provides that there are other arrangements known as trusts because the legal title to property is conveyed to trustees for the benefit of beneficiaries, but that are not classified as trusts for federal tax purposes because they are not simply arrangements to protect or conserve the property for the beneficiaries. These trusts, which are often known as business or commercial trusts, generally are created by the beneficiaries simply as a device to carry on a profit-making business that normally would have been carried on through business organizations that are classified as corporations or partnerships.

Section 301.7701-4(c)(1) provides that an "investment" trust will not be classified as a trust if there is a power under the trust agreement to vary the investment of the certificate holders. See Comm'r v. North American bond trust, 122 f.2d 545 (2d Cir. 1941), cert. Denied, 314 U.S. 701 (1942). An investment trust with a single class of ownership interests, representing undivided beneficial interests in the assets of the trust, will be classified as a trust if there is no power to vary the investment of the certificate holders. A power to vary the investment of the certificate holders exists where there is a managerial power, under the trust instrument, that enables a trust to take advantage of variations in the market to improve the investment of the investors. See Comm'r v. North American bond trust, 122 f.2d at 546.

Rev. Rul. 75-192, 1975-1 C.B. 384, discusses the situation where a provision in the trust agreement requires the trustee to invest cash on hand between the quarterly distribution dates. The trustee is required to invest the money in short-term obligations of (or guaranteed by) the United States, or any agency or instrumentality thereof, and in certificates of deposit of any bank or trust company having a minimum stated surplus and capital. The trustee is permitted to invest only in obligations maturing prior to the next distribution date and is required to hold such obligations until maturity. Rev. Rul. 75-192 concludes that, because the restrictions on the types of permitted investments limit the trustee to a fixed return similar to that earned on a bank account and eliminate any opportunity to profit from market fluctuations, the power to invest in the specified kinds of short-term investments is not a power to vary the trust's investment.

Rev. Rul. 78-371, 1978-2 C.B. 344, concludes that a trust established by the heirs of a number of contiguous parcels of real estate is an association taxable as a corporation for federal tax purposes where the trustees have the power to purchase and sell contiguous or adjacent real estate, accept or retain contributions of contiguous or adjacent real estate, raze or erect any building or structure, make any improvements to the land originally contributed, borrow money, and mortgage or lease the property. Compare rev. Rul. 79-77, 1979-1 C.B. 448 (concluding that a trust formed by three parties to hold a single parcel of real estate is classified as a trust for federal income tax purposes when the trustee has limited powers that do not evidence an intent to carry on a profit making business).

Rev. Rul. 92-105, 1992-2 C.B. 204, addresses the transfer of a taxpayer's interest in an Illinois land trust under section 1031. Under the facts of the ruling, a single taxpayer created an Illinois land trust and named a domestic corporation as trustee. Under the deed of trust, the taxpayer transferred legal and equitable title to real property to the trust, subject to the provisions of an accompanying land trust agreement. The land trust agreement provided that the taxpayer retained exclusive control of the management, operation, renting, and selling of the real property, together with an exclusive right to the earnings and proceeds from the real property. Under the agreement, the taxpayer was required to file all tax returns, pay all taxes, and satisfy any other liabilities with respect to the real property. Rev. Rul. 92-105 concludes that, because the trustee's only responsibility was to hold and transfer title at the direction of the taxpayer, a trust, as defined in section 301.7701-4(a), was not established. Moreover, there were no other arrangements between the taxpayer and the trustee (or between the taxpayer and any other person) that would cause the overall arrangement to be classified as a partnership (or any other type of entity). Instead, the trustee was a mere agent for the holding and transfer of title to real property, and the taxpayer retained direct ownership of the real property for federal income tax purposes.

Analysis

Under Delaware law, DST is an entity that is recognized as separate from its owners. Creditors of the beneficial owners of DST may not assert claims directly against Blackacre. DST may sue or be sued, and the property of DST is subject to attachment and execution as if it were a corporation. The beneficial owners of DST are entitled to the same limitation on personal liability because of actions of DST that is extended to stockholders of Delaware corporations. DST may merge or consolidate with or into one or more statutory entities or other business entities. DST is formed for investment purposes. Thus, DST is an entity for federal tax purposes.

Whether DST or its trustee is an agent of DST's beneficial owners depends upon the arrangement between the parties. The beneficiaries of DST do not enter into an agency agreement with DST or its trustee. Further, neither DST nor its trustee acts as an agent for A, B or C in dealings with third parties. Thus, neither DST nor its trustee is the agent of DST's beneficial owners. Cf. Comm'r v. Bollinger, 485 U.S. 340 (1988).

This situation is distinguishable from rev. Rul. 92-105. First, in rev. Rul. 92-105, the beneficiary retained the direct obligation to pay liabilities and taxes relating to the property. DST, in contrast, assumed a's obligations on the lease with Z and on the loan with BK, and Delaware law provides the beneficial owners of DST with the same limitation on personal liability extended to shareholders of Delaware corporations. Second, unlike a, the beneficiary in rev. Rul. 92-105 retained the right to manage and control the trust property.

Issue 1. Classification of Delaware Statutory Trust
Because DST is an entity separate from its owner, DST is either a trust or a business entity for federal tax purposes. To determine whether DST is a trust or a business entity for federal tax purposes, it is necessary, under section 301.7701-4(c)(1), to determine whether there is a power under the trust agreement to vary the investment of the certificate holders.

Prior to, but on the same date as, the transfer of Blackacre to DST, a entered into a 10-year nonrecourse loan secured by Blackacre. A also entered into the 10-year net lease agreement with Z. A's rights and obligations under the loan and lease were assumed by DST. Because the duration of DST is 10 years (unless Blackacre is disposed of prior to that time), the financing and leasing arrangements related to Blackacre that were made prior to the inception of DST are fixed for the entire life of DST. Further, the trustee may only invest in short-term obligations that mature prior to the next distribution date and is required to hold these obligations until maturity. Because the trust agreement requires that any cash from Blackacre, and any cash earned on short-term obligations held by DST between distribution dates, be distributed quarterly, and because the disposition of Blackacre results in the termination of DST, no reinvestment of such monies is possible.

The trust agreement provides that the trustee's activities are limited to the collection and distribution of income. The trustee may not exchange Blackacre for other property, purchase assets other than the short-term investments described above, or accept additional contributions of assets (including money) to DST. The trustee may not renegotiate the terms of the debt used to acquire Blackacre and may not renegotiate the lease with Z or enter into leases with tenants other than Z, except in the case of Z's bankruptcy or insolvency. In addition, the trustee may make only minor non-structural modifications to Blackacre, unless otherwise required by law.

This situation is distinguishable from rev. Rul. 78-371, because DST's trustee has none of the powers described in rev. Rul. 78-371, which evidence an intent to carry on a profit making business. Because all of the interests in DST are of a single class representing undivided beneficial interests in the assets of DST and DST's trustee has no power to vary the investment of the certificate holders to benefit from variations in the market, DST is an investment trust that will be classified as a trust under section 301.7701-4(c)(1).

Issue 2. Exchange of real property for interests under section 1031

B and C are treated as grantors of the trust under section 1.671-2(e)(3) when they acquire their interests in the trust from A. Because they have the right to distributions of all trust income attributable to their undivided fractional interests in the trust, B and C are each treated, by reason of section 677, as the owner of an aliquot portion of the trust and all income, deductions, and credits attributable to that portion are includible by B and C under section 671 in computing their taxable income. Because the owner of an undivided fractional interest of a trust is considered to own the trust assets attributable to that interest for federal income tax purposes, B and C are each considered to own an undivided fractional interest in Blackacre for federal income tax purposes. See rev. Rul. 85-13.

Accordingly, the exchange of real property by B and C for an interest in DST through a qualified intermediary is the exchange of real property for an interest in Blackacre, and not the exchange of real property for a certificate of trust or beneficial interest under section 1031(a)(2)(e). Because Whiteacre and Greenacre are of like kind to Blackacre, and provided the other requirements of section 1031 are satisfied, the exchange of real property for an interest in DST by B and C will qualify for nonrecognition of gain or loss under section 1031. Moreover, because DST is a grantor trust, the outcome to the parties will remain the same, even if a transfers interests in Blackacre directly to B and C, and B and C immediately form DST by contributing their interests in Blackacre.

Under the facts of this case, if DST's trustee has additional powers under the trust agreement such as the power to do one or more of the following: (i) dispose of Blackacre and acquire new property; (ii) renegotiate the lease with Z or enter into leases with tenants other than Z; (iii) renegotiate or refinance the obligation used to purchase Blackacre; (iv) invest cash received to profit from market fluctuations; or (v) make more than minor non-structural modifications to Blackacre not required by law, DST will be a business entity which, if it has two or more owners, will be classified as a partnership for federal tax purposes, unless it is treated as a corporation under section 7704 or elects to be classified as a corporation under section 301.7701-3. In addition, because the assets of DST will not be owned by the beneficiaries as co-owners under state law, DST will not be able to elect to be excluded from the application of subchapter k. See section 1.761-2(a)(2)(i).

Holdings
(1) The Delaware Statutory Trust described above is an investment trust, under section 301.7701-4(c), that will be classified as a trust for federal tax purposes.

(2) A taxpayer may exchange real property for an interest in the Delaware Statutory Trust described above without recognition of gain or loss under section 1031, if the other requirements of section 1031 are satisfied.

Appendix III

Rev. Proc. 2002-22

Section 1. Purpose

This revenue procedure specifies the conditions under which the internal revenue service will consider a request for a ruling that an undivided fractional interest in rental real property (other than a mineral property as defined in section 614) is not an interest in a business entity, within the meaning of 301.7701-2(a) of the procedure and administration regulations. This revenue procedure supersedes rev. Proc. 2000-46, 2002-2 C.B. 438, which provides that the service will not issue advance rulings or determination letters on the questions of whether an undivided fractional interest in real property is an interest in an entity that is not eligible for tax-free exchange under section 1031(a)(1) of the internal revenue code and whether arrangements where taxpayers acquire undivided fractional interests in real property constitute separate entities for federal tax purposes under section 7701. This revenue procedure also modifies rev. Proc. 2002-3, 2002-1 I.R.B. 117, by removing these issues from the list of subjects on which the service will not rule. Requests for 1 advance rulings described in rev. Proc. 2000-46 that are not covered by this revenue procedure, such as rulings concerning mineral property, will be considered under procedures set forth in Rev. Proc. 2002-1, 2002-1 I.R.B. 1 (or its successor).

Section 2. Background section

301.7701-1(a)(1) provides that whether an organization is an entity separate from its owners for federal tax purposes is a matter of federal law and does not depend on whether the entity is recognized as an entity under local law. Section 301.7701-1(a)(2) provides that a joint venture or other contractual arrangement may create a separate entity for federal tax purposes if the participants carry on a trade, business, financial operation, or venture and divide the profits therefrom, but the mere co-ownership of property that is maintained, kept in repair, and rented or leased does not constitute a separate entity for federal tax purposes. Section 301.7701-2(a) provides that a business entity is any entity recognized for federal tax purposes (including an entity with a single owner that may be disregarded as an entity separate from its owner under 301.7701-3) that is not properly classified as a trust under 301.7701-4 or otherwise subject to special treatment under the internal revenue code. A business entity with two or more members is classified for federal tax purposes as either a corporation or a partnership. 2 Section 761(a) provides that the term partnership includes a syndicate, group, pool, joint venture, or other unincorporated organization through or by means of which any business, financial operation, or venture is carried on, and that is not a corporation or a trust or estate. Section 1.761-1(a) of the income tax regulations provides that the term partnership means a partnership as determined under 301.7701-1, 301.7701-2, and 301.7701-3. The central characteristic of a tenancy in common, one of the traditional concurrent estates in land, is that each owner is deemed to own individually a physically undivided part of the entire parcel of property. Each tenant in common is entitled to share with the other tenants the possession of the whole parcel and has the associated rights to a proportionate share of rents or profits from the property, to transfer the interest, and to demand a partition of the property. These rights generally provide a tenant in common the benefits of ownership of the property within the constraint that no rights may be exercised to the detriment of the other tenants in common. 7 Richard R. Powell, Powell on real property 50.01-50.07 (Michael Allan Wolf ed., 2000). Rev. Rul. 75-374, 1975-2 C.B. 261, concludes that a two-person co-ownership of an apartment building that was rented to tenants did not constitute a partnership for federal tax purposes. In the revenue ruling, the co-owners employed an agent to manage the apartments on their behalf; the agent collected rents, paid property taxes, insurance premiums, repair and maintenance expenses, and provided the tenants with customary services, such as heat, air conditioning, trash removal, unattended parking, and maintenance of public areas. The ruling concludes that the agent's activities in providing customary services to the tenants, although imputed to the co-owners, were not sufficiently extensive to cause the co-ownership to be characterized as a partnership. See also rev. Rul. 79-77, 1979-1 C.B. 448, which did not find a business entity WH individuals transferred ownership of a commercial building subject to a net lease to a trust with the three individuals as beneficiaries. Where a sponsor packages co-ownership interests for sale by acquiring property, negotiating a master lease on the property, and arranging for financing, the courts have looked at the relationships not only among the co-owners, but also between the sponsor (or persons related to the sponsor) and the co-owners in determining whether the coownership gives rise to a partnership. For example, in Bergford v. Commissioner, 12 f.3d 166 (9th Cir. 1993), 78 investors purchased co-ownership interests in computer equipment that was subject to a 7-year net lease. As part of the purchase, the co-owners authorized the manager to arrange financing and refinancing, purchase and lease the equipment, collect rents and apply those rents to the notes used to finance the equipment, prepare statements, and advance funds to participants on an interest-free basis to meet cash flow. The agreement allowed the co-owners to decide by majority vote whether to sell or lease the equipment at the end of the lease. Absent a majority vote, the manager could make that decision. In addition, the manager was entitled to a remarketing fee of 10 percent of the equipment's selling price or lease rental whether or not a coowner terminated the agreement or the manager performed any remarketing. A co-owner could assign an interest in the co-ownership only after fulfilling numerous conditions and obtaining the manager's consent. The court held that the co-ownership arrangement constituted a partnership for federal tax purposes. Among the factors that influenced the court's decision were the limitations on the co-owners' ability to sell, lease or encumber either the co-ownership 4 interest or the underlying property, and the manager's effective participation in both profits (through the remarketing fee) and losses (through the advances). Bergford, 12 f.3d at 169-170. Accord bussing v. Commissioner, 88 T.C. 449 (1987), affd on rehg, 89 T.C. 1050 (1987); Alhouse v. Commissioner, T.C. memo. 1991-652. Under 1.761-1(a) and 301.7701-1 through 301.7701-3, a federal tax partnership does not include mere co-ownership of property where the owners' activities are limited to keeping the property maintained, in repair, rented or leased. However, as the above authorities demonstrate, a partnership for federal tax purposes is broader in scope than the common law meaning of partnership and may include groups not classified by state law as partnerships. Bergford, 12 f.3d at 169. Where the parties to a venture join together capital or services with the intent of conducting a business or enterprise and of sharing the profits and losses from the venture, a partnership (or other business entity) is created. Bussing, 88 T.C. at 460. Furthermore, where the economic benefits to the individual participants are not derivative of their co-ownership, but rather come from their joint relationship toward a common goal, the co-ownership arrangement will be characterized as a partnership (or other business entity) for federal tax purposes. Bergford, 12 f.3d at 169.

Section 3. Scope
This revenue procedure applies to co-ownership of rental real property (other than mineral interests) (the property) in an arrangement classified under local law as a tenancy-in-common.

5 this revenue procedure provides guidelines for requesting advance rulings solely to assist taxpayers in preparing ruling requests and the service in issuing advance ruling letters as promptly as practicable. The guidelines set forth in this revenue procedure are not intended to be substantive rules and are not to be used for audit purposes.

Section 4. Guidelines for submitting ruling requests
The service ordinarily will not consider a request for a ruling under this a single business unit where there is a close connection between the business use of one parcel and the business use of another parcel. For example, an office building and a garage that services the tenants of the office building may be treated as a single business unit even if the office building and the garage are not contiguous. For purposes of this revenue procedure, the following definitions apply. The term co-owner means any person that owns an interest in the property as a tenant in common. The term sponsor means any person who divides a single interest in the property into multiple co-ownership interests for the purpose of offering those interests for sale. The term related person means a person bearing a relationship described in 267(b) or 707(b)(1), except that in applying 267(b) or 707(b)(1), the co-ownership will be treated as a partnership and each co-owner will be treated as a partner. The term "disregarded entity" means an entity that is disregarded as an entity separate from its owner for federal tax purposes. Examples of disregarded entities include qualified REIT subsidiaries (within the meaning of 856(i)(2)), qualified subchapter s subsidiaries (within the meaning of 1361(b)(3)(b)), and business entities that have only one owner and do not elect to be classified as corporations. The term blanket lien means any mortgage or trust deed that is recorded against the property as a whole.

Section 5. Information to be submitted
.01 Section 8 of rev. Proc. 2002-1 outlines general requirements

concerning the information to be submitted as part of a ruling request, including advance rulings under this revenue procedure. For example, any ruling request must contain a complete statement of all facts relating to the co-ownership, including those relating to promoting, 7 financing and managing the property. Among the information to be included are the items of information specified in this revenue procedure; therefore, the ruling request must provide all items of information and conditions specified below and in section 6 of this revenue procedure, or at least account for all of the items. For example, if a co-ownership arrangement has no brokerage agreement permitted in section 6.12 of this revenue procedure, the ruling request should so state. Furthermore, merely submitting documents and supplementary materials required by section 5.02 of this revenue procedure does not satisfy all of the information requirements contained in section 5.02 of this revenue procedure or in section 8 of Rev. Proc. 2002-1; all material facts in the documents submitted must be explained in the ruling request and may not be merely incorporated by reference. All submitted documents and supplementary materials must contain applicable exhibits, attachments, and amendments. The ruling request must identify and explain any information or documents required in section 5 of this revenue procedure that are not included and any conditions in section 6 of this revenue procedure that are or are not satisfied.

.02 Required general information and copies of documents and supplementary materials.
Generally the following information and copies of documents and materials must be submitted with the ruling request: (1) the name, taxpayer identification number, and percentage fractional interest in property of each co-owner; 8 (2) the name, taxpayer identification number, ownership of, and any relationship among, all persons involved in the acquisition, sale,

lease and other use of property, including the sponsor, lessee, manager, and lender; (3) a full description of the property; (4) a representation that each of the co-owners holds title to the property (including each of multiple parcels of property treated as a single property under this revenue procedure) as a tenant in common under local law; (5) all promotional documents relating to the sale of fractional interests in the property; (6) all lending agreements relating to the property; (7) all agreements among the co-owners relating to the property; (8) any lease agreement relating to the property; (9) any purchase and sale agreement relating to the property; (10) any property management or brokerage agreement relating to the property; and (11) any other agreement relating to the property not specified in this section, including agreements relating to any debt secured by the property (such as guarantees or indemnity agreements) and any call and put options relating to the property.

Section 6. Conditions for obtaining rulings
The service ordinarily will not consider a request for a ruling under this revenue procedure unless the conditions described below are satisfied. Nevertheless, where the conditions described below are not satisfied, the service may consider a request for a 9 ruling under this revenue procedure where the facts and circumstances clearly establish that such a ruling is appropriate.

.01 Tenancy in common ownership. Each of the co-owners must hold title to the property (either directly or through a disregarded entity) as a tenant in common under local law. Thus, title to the property as a whole may not be held by an entity recognized under local law.

.02 Number of co-owners. The number of co-owners must be limited to no more than 35 persons. For this purpose, person is defined as in 7701(a)(1), except that a husband and wife are treated as a single person and all persons who acquire interests from a co-owner by inheritance are treated as a single person.

.03 No treatment of co-ownership as an entity. The co-ownership may not file a partnership or corporate tax return, conduct business under a common name, execute an agreement identifying any or all of the co-owners as partners, shareholders or members of a business entity, or otherwise hold itself out as a partnership or other form of business entity (nor may the co-owners hold themselves out as partners, shareholders, or members of a business entity). The service generally will not issue a ruling under this revenue procedure if the co-owners held interests in the property through a partnership or corporation immediately prior to the formation of the co-ownership.

.04 Co-ownership agreement. The co-owners may enter into a limited co-ownership agreement that may run with the land. For example, a co-ownership agreement may provide that a co-owner must offer the co-ownership interest for sale to the other co-owners, the sponsor, or the lessee at fair market value (determined as of the 10 time the partition right is exercised) before exercising any right to partition (see section 6.06 of this revenue procedure for conditions relating to restrictions on alienation); or that certain actions on behalf of the co-ownership require the vote of co-owners holding more than 50 percent of the undivided interests in the property (see section 6.05 of this revenue procedure for conditions relating to voting).

.05 Voting. The co-owners must retain the right to approve the hiring of any manager, the sale or other disposition of the property, any leases of a portion or all of the property, or the creation or modification of a blanket lien. Any sale, lease, or re-lease of a portion or all of the property, any negotiation or renegotiation of indebtedness secured by a blanket lien, the hiring of any manager, or the negotiation of any management contract (or any extension or renewal of such contract) must be by unanimous approval of the co-owners. For all other actions on behalf of the co-ownership, the co-owners may agree to be bound by the vote of those holding more than 50 percent of the undivided interests in the property. A co-owner who has consented to an action in conformance with this section 6.05 may provide the manager or other person a power of attorney to execute a specific document with respect to that action, but may not provide the manager or other person with a global power of attorney.

.06 Restrictions on alienation. In general, each co-owner must have the rights to transfer, partition, and encumber the co-owners' undivided interest in the property without the agreement or approval of any person. However, restrictions on the right to transfer, partition or encumber interests in the property that are required by a lender and that are consistent with customary commercial lending practices are not prohibited. See 11 Section 6.14 of this revenue procedure for restrictions on who may be a lender. Moreover, the co-owners, the sponsor or the lessee may have a right of first offer (the right to have the first opportunity to offer to purchase the co-ownership interest) with respect to any co-owner's exercise of the right to transfer the co-ownership interest in the property. In addition, a co-owner may agree to offer the co-ownership interest for sale to the other co-owners, the sponsor, or the lessee at fair market value (determined as of the time the partition right is exercised) before exercising any right to partition.

.07 Sharing proceeds and liabilities upon sale of property. If the property is sold, any debt secured by a blanket lien must be satisfied and the remaining sales proceeds must be distributed to the co-owners.

.08 Proportionate sharing of profits and losses. Each co-owner must share in all revenues generated by the property and all costs associated with the property in proportion to the co-owner's undivided interest in the property. Neither the other co-owners, nor the sponsor, nor the manager may advance funds to a co-owner to meet expenses associated with the co-ownership interest, unless the advance is recourse to the co-owner (and, where the co-owner is a disregarded entity, the owner of the co-owner) and is not for a period exceeding 31 days.

.09 Proportionate sharing of debt. The co-owners must share in any indebtedness secured by a blanket lien in proportion to their undivided interests.

.10 Options. A co-owner may issue an option to purchase the co-owner's undivided interest (call option), provided that the exercise price for the call option reflects the fair market value of the property determined as of the time the option is exercised. 12 for this purpose, the fair market value of an undivided interest in the property is equal to the co-owner's percentage interest in the property multiplied by the fair market value of the property as a whole. A co-owner may not acquire an option to sell the co-owner's undivided interest (put option) to the sponsor, the lessee, another co-owner, or the lender, or any person related to the sponsor, the lessee, another co-owner, or the lender.

.11 No business activities. The co-owners' activities must be limited to those customarily performed in connection with the maintenance and repair of rental real property (customary activities). See rev. Rul. 75-374, 1975-2 C.B. 261. Activities will be treated as customary activities for this purpose if the activities would not prevent an amount received by an organization described in 511(a)(2) from qualifying as rent under 512(b)(3)(a) and the regulations thereunder. In determining the co-owners' activities, all activities of the co-owners, their agents and any persons related to the co-owners with respect to the property will be taken into account, whether or not those activities are performed by the co-owners in their capacities as co-owners. For example, if the sponsor or a lessee is a co-owner, then all of the activities of the sponsor or lessee (or any person related to the sponsor or lessee) with respect to the property will be taken into account in determining whether the co-owners' activities are customary activities. However, activities of a co-owner or a related person with respect to the property (other than in the co-owner's capacity as a co-owner) will not be taken into account if the co-owner owns an undivided interest in the property for less than 6 months.

.12 Management and brokerage agreements. The co-owners may enter into management or brokerage agreements, which must be renewable no less frequently than 13 annually, with an agent, who may be the sponsor or a co-owner (or any person related to the sponsor or a co-owner), but who may not be a lessee. The management agreement may authorize the manager to maintain a common bank account for the collection and deposit of rents and to offset expenses associated with the property against any revenues before disbursing each co-owner's share of net revenues. In all events, however, the manager must disburse to the co-owners their shares of net revenues within 3 months from the date of receipt of those revenues. The management agreement may also authorize the manager to prepare statements for the co-owners showing their shares of revenue and costs from the property. In addition, the management agreement may authorize the manager to obtain or modify insurance on the property, and to negotiate modifications of the terms of any lease or any indebtedness encumbering the property, subject to the approval of the co-owners. (see section 6.05 of this revenue procedure for conditions relating to the approval of lease and debt modifications.) The determination of any fees paid by the co-ownership to the manager must not depend in whole or in part on the income or profits derived by any person from the property and may not exceed the fair market value of the manager's services. Any fee paid by the co-ownership to a broker must be comparable to fees paid by unrelated parties to brokers for similar services.

.13 Leasing agreements. All leasing arrangements must be bona fide leases for federal tax purposes. Rents paid by a lessee must reflect the fair market value for the use of the property. The determination of the amount of the rent must not depend, in whole or in part, on the income or profits derived by any person from the property leased (other than an amount based on a fixed percentage or percentages of receipts or sales). See 14 section 856(d)(2)(a) and the regulations thereunder. Thus, for example, the amount of rent paid by a lessee may not be based on a percentage of net income from the property, cash flow, increases in equity or similar arrangements.

.14 Loan agreements. The lender with respect to any debt that encumbers the property or with respect to any debt incurred to acquire an undivided interest in the property may not be a related person to any co-owner, the sponsor, the manager or any lessee of the property.

.15 Payments to sponsor. Except as otherwise provided in this revenue procedure, the amount of any payment to the sponsor for the acquisition of the co-ownership interest (and the amount of any fees paid to the sponsor for services) must reflect the fair market value of the acquired co-ownership interest (or the services rendered) and may not depend, in whole or in part, on the income or profits derived by any person from the property. Section 6. Effect on other documents rev. Proc. 2000-46 is superseded. Rev. Proc. 2002-3 is modified by removing sections 5.03 and 5.06.

Section 7. Drafting information

The principal authors of this revenue procedure are Jeanne Sullivan and Deane Burke of the Office of Associate Chief Counsel (passthroughs and special industries). For further information regarding this revenue procedure, contact Ms. Sullivan or Mr. Burke at (202) 622-3070 (not a toll-free call).

Appendix IV

Risk

DST risks, fees, rules and restrictions

Investing in a beneficial ownership interest of a Delaware Statutory Trust carries many of the same risks as investing in direct ownership of real estate property. Due to the structure of the DST as a passive ownership entity, a beneficial ownership interest in a DST presents additional risks that the investor should be aware of. The following risks should be fully understood and carefully considered when assessing an investor's suitability for ownership of a Delaware Statutory Trust:

- Lack of liquidity and timing of exit – Generally DSTs have a target property hold period ranging from 3 – 10 years. The hold period may differ significantly from the targeted timeline based on market conditions. The investment should be viewed as illiquid while invested in the property. Early exit by the investor for liquidity purposes may not be possible or may be only possible at a significant discount to the trust's net asset value.

- Lack of control – Owners of a beneficial interest in Delaware Statutory Trust have little control over management decisions and eventual sale of the underlying property. The real estate investment company managing the trust is responsible for all operating decisions.

- Failure of due diligence and non-compliance – All DSTs offered through our firm are subject to a rigorous due diligence process in which the real estate investment company's management are thoroughly reviewed, as are each individual DST offerings made available.

However, failure to identify an issue may result in mis-management or non-compliance in adhering to the IRS criteria established for a DST to qualify for tax-deferred exchange treatment.

- Loan modifications may not be possible – Due to the structure of a DST, restructuring the financing of the property may not be possible without changing the legal ownership structure. DSTs mitigate this issue by utilizing master lease agreements between the trust and the real estate investment company.

- Projected cash flow may not be consistent with actual performance – As with any real estate property invest-ment, cash flow levels are subject to market, econom-ic, tenant and location risk. Projected cash flows are typically conservative in nature; however, they are not guaranteed.

- Projected appreciation may not occur – As with any real estate property investment, asset appreciation is subject to market, economic, tenant and location risk. Appreciation may not occur at the end of the trust's property holding period or the holding period may be extended beyond stated projections.

- Interest rate risk – The value of real estate is heavily impacted by the current interest rate environment. Changes in current interest rates may increase uncer-tainty surrounding financing, leasing and appreciation.

- Regulatory risk – DSTs are susceptible to changes in the IRS's treatment of tax-deferred exchanges. Furthermore, the advantages of ownership of a beneficial interest in a DST for estate planning purposes may be eliminated based on changes in the internal revenue code.

- DST management costs and fees – DST structure provides for management fees to the sponsoring real estate investment company. These fees, while thoroughly disclosed upfront could serve to reduce cash-flow levels below that of the stated projections.

It is our highest priority to educate our clients to the potential risks and uncertainties regarding ownership of Delaware Statutory Trusts. All DST properties presented to clients will be accompanied by a Private Placement Memorandum. This full disclosure document will provide detailed information on all relevant matters pertaining to the DST include risk disclosures. If you may be ready to give up your landlord responsibilities and are considering moving up to a passive real estate owner, contact us with any questions about a beneficial interest in a DST.